A Homemade

A Mother's Guide to Slow, Simple, & Seasonal Homeschooling

CW00540880

Copyright

A Homemade Education: A mother's guide to slow, simple, & seasonal homeschooling. Copyright © 2024 by Shelby Dersa. All rights reserved. No part of this book may be used or reproduced in any manner whatsoever without written permission. The author and publisher assumes no responsibility for errors, inaccuracies, omissions, or advice given in this book.

For information, please email ahomemadeeducation@gmail.com or visit http://ahomemadeeducationpress.com

Paperback edition published by A Homemade Education Press in 2024.

Designed by: Shelby Dersa
Cover art by: Sandra Dersa
Interior illustrations by: Melissa Loxton & Canva
Interior photography by: Shelby Dersa & Canva

ISBN 979-8-9882547-2-0

Dedication

For my husband, who has created this perfect life with me. For my children, who are my reasons for living.

Table of Contents

Give me a quiet life.
One where I can hear the trees rustling in the wind, raindrops on the windows, pages of a book turning, coffee being brewed, and the heartbeats of the ones I love.

Chapter 1

Craving a Simple Life

How wonderful would it be to live slowly with our children?

To let them wake when their little bodies are well-rested? To make a warm breakfast just because you have the time? Cuddles, crafts, and hide and seek could fill up the days ahead. Afternoon walks in the sun. More stories, talks, and hugs. How wonderful would it be?

This is the kind of life that many crave for their children, yet most are either too afraid to go after or do not know how to make the necessary adjustments. American culture has been slowly, but steadily altering the lives of children, going from simple and magical to fast, busy, and materialistic. One of the most dramatic impacts is due to the rise of technological advances. Today, many children are lacking an appreciation for life's simple pleasures, nature, and human connection.

Family life is also put on the back burner due to the lack of time within the average household. Parents are influenced to believe that children should almost always be busy. The thought is that they should be constantly moving from one activity to the next. With the seven hours that a child attends a traditional school, plus after-school activities and homework, they often lack free time before having to settle down for bed. The stress and anxiety that many children face are real, yet our culture acts as if they can handle it and expects them to keep persevering regardless. Those "stomach aches" children and adolescents complain of in the early mornings before school are often not to fake sick or to be deceptive with their parents. In many cases, they could simply be crying out for a break. How often do you think their parents listen?

The education system plays a large role in convincing parents that a child's mind should be overflowed with too much information to memorize or ever use. The knowledge that children absorb is constantly being tested, checked, and graded. It doesn't matter if little Susie loves books, has phenomenal comprehension skills in reading, or has a large vocabulary for her age, if she is also not great at math. No one cares if eight-year-old Jonny can do amazing things with his hands, such as setting up conductors to turn on a light bulb, if he can't sit still for hours at a time without being fidgety. If a child does not measure up to a school's standards in any way, shape, or form, then that is what is recorded on report cards or talked about during conferences. When homeschooling, past beliefs of what a good education should look like may be embedded in a mother's thoughts, which may mistakenly cause her to copy a regular classroom setup instead of realizing that her children can be free from that environment.

Practical skills, imaginative play, hands-on learning, reading good books, positive social skills, self-directed learning, and outdoor exploration are lacking in schools across the country. We are told that those types of learning experiences are the responsibility of the parent when children are at home. But when you stop to think about it, when is there enough time for the average family to do those things? Families are lucky to eat a good dinner together, get homework done, and accomplish other necessary tasks that the day requires. In our society, it's understandable that mothers are afraid of being judged for choosing a path for their children that is out of the ordinary, but when it comes down to it, you can never go wrong when choosing the well-being of your family over society's expectations.

Homeschool Intentionally

You may be familiar with the term "intentional living," which is the act of spending one's day purposefully. This doesn't mean that every day is occupied with exciting things to do or places to go because you recognize that life is short. It doesn't have anything to do with buying more or a "go big or go home" attitude.

Intentional living is realizing that every ordinary moment in our lives is meaningful, and should be done with gratitude, passion, and purpose. From the things we do, the knowledge we consume, and the entertainment we use, to the attitudes and words we give to other people, they can all be done more intentionally. So what does all of this have to do with homeschooling? Everything! Chances are, you have decided to homeschool because you want a more fulfilling education for your child or a more fulfilling life in general.

As homeschool mothers, we have the ability to craft a homemade education. One that does not drain their souls, but fills them up. A learning atmosphere that is not separated from normal life, but is intertwined. We recognize the importance of slowing down and letting children be unbusy. We know that something special could be waiting for them that lies outside of the school building, secured with tall fences. Home is a place where a different set of principles are able to be instilled. As a result, children can have a chance to reap the rewards of a restored childhood.

As Soon As He Turns Three

They want to send my child off to school
As soon as he turns three.
They think he'll be more successful there
Instead of at home with me.
They want to send my child off to school
But they don't know him like I do.
They say he'll learn better with teachers
But I don't think that's true.
They want to send my child off to school
Where he can thrive and grow.
But I think he'll learn best
Where he has been planted and sown.
They want to send my child off to school
So he can fit in with everyone else.
But maybe I don't want him to,
Maybe I'd rather him stand out.
They want to send my child off to school
Where he can get the tools to succeed.
But how do they give him that
If they can't change anything to fit his needs?
They want to send my child off to school
So he can socialize with others.
They say it's not good enough
To be with his sister and brother.
They want to send my child off to school
So he can get out of the house to explore.
They have no idea about all that we do..
Parks, libraries, play groups, and the outdoors.
They want to send my child off to school
When he is only three.
They have no idea that homeschooling brings
Wonder, joy, and a child who feels free.

In a world full of moms who are living rushed and busy lives, live simply, slowly, and lovely instead.

Chapter 2

A Lovely & Intentional Motherhood

Throughout all four seasons, during each day, and down to every moment, mothers are given an opportunity to live life intentionally by preparing an environment that promotes less rushing, creates warm memories, embraces simplicity, and pursues meaningful skills and knowledge for not only her family but also for themselves. While it's true that you are creating their childhood, you are also creating your motherhood. Make it beautiful.

The Mother's Soul

You are a woman with your own needs, wants, and desires. When your cup is running dry, you can't happily serve others. Not only should you search for ways to live intentionally with your children or partner, but you should look to fuel yourself as well.

Have you ever gone through one of those ruts where dressing up didn't happen for many days at a time? Maybe it was when you weren't feeling the best about your body, your current wardrobe, or were just too mentally drained to care? Sometimes, life feels easier when we go through these periods. After all, it does save plenty of time not styling your hair or waking up early to put on makeup. Grabbing your comfiest clothes out of the closet without having to think about what you'll wear takes less effort too. But what happened when a day came where you felt the need to get a little dolled up or to look your best, such as for a special occasion? You likely could've felt a rush of confidence run through your body that day. For some reason, women, and even people in general, feel good when they look good. I don't know if there's any scientific evidence to back that notion up, but I do know I feel it too. It's not about being conceited or "too concerned with looks." Taking the time to go the extra mile and add those special touches to yourself on most days will shift your mood and can set you up for a better day ahead.

Keeping your soul fueled takes some effort in other ways as well. Taking time to pursue interests or discover a new passion can go a long way and should be made into one of your priorities. I have found that picking one simple thing every once in a while that I would like to try can keep life exciting. It doesn't have to be anything wild either. Whether you're into learning how to bake bread, embroider, kayak, write poetry, refinish old furniture, or dry flowers, any activity can be beneficial. The first way to get started is to declare that you are going to do it.

Even though homeschool mothers are very busy inside of their homes and with their families, finding ways to give back to others should not be looked over. Whether you enjoy jumping into larger volunteer roles in your community or prefer smaller acts of kindness, doing so is good for the soul. Leading a class at your local homeschool cooperative, organizing your own small homeschool group, volunteering at your church's Sunday school, doing some chores for an elderly neighbor, or dropping off dinner to a new mother are all examples.

Being an adult and having a family means less time for friendships, but making a point to meet up with a friend every once in a blue moon could leave you feeling refreshed after having good conversations and catching up. If getting out of the house is too hard, invite them over for coffee. If neither of you have time available away from the kids, set up a playdate. Life is shorter than we think. Don't let too much time go by without seeing someone who is special to you.

The Mother's Mind

Even though it sometimes feels like our brains are fried due to living life as a mother, taking care of our homes, meal planning/cooking, keeping our relationships going, keeping our partners happy, and to top it off, homeschooling, we have a beautiful mind that should be taken care of too.

Being spiritualistic, religious, or "one with nature," are what some women identify themselves as. If you do not, that's fine too, but I think it is worth noting since these aspects of a mother's life are important to many and shouldn't be skipped over for the sake of those specific mothers. Oftentimes, these things shape our beliefs and behaviors. If any of them are a part of your life, I encourage you to make time for them, as they can be healing to the mind and have a positive effect on your attitude.

Speaking of attitudes, they can be affected and altered so easily over the course of a day, can't they? You might feel good when you wake up, but one bad thing could happen that propels you into feeling annoyed the rest of the morning and pouring onto the people around you. Don't get me wrong though, just because we are mothers who may be surrounded by the people we love, doesn't mean we aren't allowed to become upset or let our feelings out sometimes. After all, we are human too. Like all humans, though, everyone has room for improvement. If your attitude is easily affected, you may want to be mindful of that and how it could sabotage your own contentment and also shift the mood in your entire household, which I'm sure most mothers do not deliberately want.

Filling up our children's minds with knowledge is usually a homeschool mother's sole focus when it comes to education, but we shouldn't stop filling our own minds just because we are older and not in school anymore. If mothers want to teach their children to be life-long learners, then remembering to model these habits is important. Not only should it be done for that reason though, but because you are deserving of new information, skills, and thoughts on worldly matters too. Keep your brain stimulated by making time to learn something new as often as you can, whether it's through books, videos, or by joining a group of individuals who are learning the same skill.

The Mother's Parenting

This section is not an opportunity for me to tell you how to be a parent. Everyone's parenting style is different. We live in a world where mothers are constantly being judged, mainly because of the use of social media. People are so quick to shame others, talk about what they think is right or wrong, or to give opinions on how they would handle a certain situation.

Have you noticed how almost anything can be turned into an argument about parenting? Recently, there was a new trend going around where a parent unexpectedly cracks an egg over their child's head and films their reaction. Some kids cried, others laughed, and a few jokingly threatened to pull a prank of their own to get even. After these videos started to appear online, many adults rushed to the comment sections to release their fury about how it was mean to do that to their kids just for likes. Some individuals thought it was harmless and funny, while others screamed child abuse. Personally, I did not care for it, but accusing parents of child abuse seems extreme. That's how a lot of situations seem to be these days. People either think parents are doing it right or are doing it wrong. How about minding our own business unless something serious really is happening? We would want others to show us the same grace, especially during our not-so-great moments with our kids.

The only style of parenting that I like to encourage others to try is "intentional parenting." It doesn't involve changing all of your ways of doing things or striving to be a perfect mother. Intentional parenting is learning ways to parent with purpose and applying some of them to your daily lives whenever *you* want to. It's about realizing that as a mother, you are the curator of their childhood. You are the one who can show them the joys of a simple life. Teach them to appreciate what is around them, practice slow living, and don't rush through life with them. Things like letting children help bake, even though it may take longer, or getting out the glitter, even though it will make a mess. Going for a walk and pointing out interesting things to look at, reading lots of stories, and singing songs often are all examples of parenting intentionally. Is it possible to always be this present with your children? Of course not, but it can be a nice intention to always have on your mind and ready to use when you are able to.

A Wise Woman Builds Her Home

Isn't it a wonderful thought that women are the makers of their homes? Whether she works outside of it or not, every woman makes her house what it is. Without them, most homes would be just a structure held up by beams and boards.

When a woman becomes a mother, those skills that she was born with go on full display. Mothers have a special gift where they are able to make any house a home. It doesn't matter how little money one has. A bare cupboard turns into a hearty supper, old walls become a beautiful canvas, and a second-hand tree doesn't prevent a magical holiday on Christmas morning. Instead of comparing men and women by saying "fathers can do that too!", let us celebrate mothers by taking notice of these qualities.

Just as easily as a mother can build her home, though, she can tear it down with her own hands. Neglect occurs when a mother puts too many other needs before herself, family and household. This can sometimes happen without even realizing it. Maybe you slowly get wrapped up in other projects, add too many things to your family's schedule, or have a hard time saying no to the people outside of your home far too often. For many, it takes a breaking point to realize that you have too much going on and the things that matter most are being neglected, including your inner peace. For mothers, it can feel like we aren't doing enough if we aren't doing it all. Keep in mind that every day doesn't need to be busy in order to feel accomplished. A slow day at home often accomplishes more than our busiest day out.

Procrastination is something else that may get the best of us. It can come and go or may be a consistent pattern for you. Other people in your life might have come to know you as the one who is always late, a last-minute planner, or is often frazzled. The people who it affects the most though are the ones in your own home. I remember when I was a young mom with a baby and a preschooler. Waking early enough in the morning to feed, clothe, and get out of the house was always stressful. Yelling at my daughter to hurry up and running around the house like a chicken with it's head cut off was preventing us from having a peaceful morning and ruining the experiences of any activity we had planned for that day. Years later, I had one more child and did a lot of growing up since the first two children were born. I knew that I didn't want history to repeat itself, so I put in the work to not let that happen as often as I could. The moral of this story is: wake up earlier, not just for our own peace, but for our family's also. In doing so, we find that the stress of rushing does not come to exist and the morning can start slowly, laying the foundation for the rest of our day.

A mother who manages her resources and uses her skills wisely has a rich family. A mother who doesn't, has a family that will never have enough. Always looking for ways to save money, being thrifty, or recycling items that you already have are important in order for a home and the people in it to have everything they need. If financial problems are not currently an issue, unexpected situations can change overnight, so it's smart not to waste resources foolishly. Your children also may not have the same financial situation as you when they grow up, so being a resourceful mother and modeling that to your children will be beneficial. Not making use of your own skills is also a waste of resources. Buying something brand new when you can fix, mend, or make it yourself are examples. Not to say people should never buy anything new, but putting in some effort not to can go a long way.

Lastly, a mother should never ignore her unique abilities or strengths, but should take advantage of them fully. Aside from being an important contribution to her household, they are part of what makes one so special to her family. When you think of your own mom, grandmother, or even another role model in your past, can you remember anything that they did well? You may have memories of them putting their talents to use in a way that benefited your family. Maybe that person is the one you turned to when you needed help with a certain task or advice. It may seem insignificant in your daily life right now, but those little things leave a lasting impact on others around you.

My grandma is known for her hamburger soup that she

 would make from four ingredients and have enough leftovers to last for days. When I was a kid who was faced with

anxiety about something going on in my life, my mom wasn't the type to say things like "oh you'll be fine." She would actually really talk to me about what was bothering me and help me through it. To this day, I can still call her when I'm worried about something, and she'll talk me through it just as she has always done.

When you go through your normal day-to-day routine, don't ever feel like what you do is insignificant, for it is the little things that make up the biggest part of life. The ones close to you will notice, either now or after you're gone.

An Enchanting Motherhood

It's no secret that when a woman becomes a mother, the single greatest thing that she loses (besides sleep) is her free time. Those times when you could scroll on your phone, read a book, or sit on the porch for hours while sipping your coffee on a saturday afternoon are the simple things that we often didn't realize we took for granted before a baby came along. Mothers might get lost during these days, and I'm sure that many become depressed as well. What a lot of women fail to realize is that they are simply stuck between their old lives and their new ones. Nothing can change the fact that they are a mother, but they can change how they look at being one. Motherhood does not have to be dull, basic, or boring. Women are usually born with the ability to make anything magical; they just have to hone in on it for the sake of themselves. This quality allows them to be able to romanticize their lives in a way that embraces everyday tasks and routines. If practiced regularly, women have the chance to be happier, more calm, satisfied, and even grateful.

Ways to Romanticize Motherhood

Utilize the Outdoors
- Choose to drink your coffee on the patio
- Take your kids on a picnic instead of a regular lunch
- Create your very own nature journal
- Hang up a bird feeder and enjoy watching the birds
- Water your flowers joyfully
- Make and tend a garden, even if it is very small
- Go on more walks
- Open a window more often for fresh air
- Take school outside if weather allows it
- Set a goal for both yourself and your children to be outside more
- Visit a park you've never been to before

Add Mood Lighting

The lighting you choose can add a warmer feel to your home with a flip of a switch or spark of a match.

- Fairy or twinkle lights
- Traditional candles, candle lamp warmers, or tea lights
- Table top lamps with soft lighting
- Himalayan salt lamps
- Moon lamps
- Christmas village houses during the holidays

Don't Believe That Chores Have to be Dull

- Pick some fresh flowers for your table
- Use a diffuser with oils to give your home a clean scent
- Try making your own detergent or other cleaners
- Hang clothes outside to dry if weather permits
- Add scented powders to your vacuum
- Get your favorite soap to do the dishes
- Open windows to freshen up your home while cleaning
- Don't be afraid to ask your kids to do chores that they can handle. Life is so much easier when you're not doing it all alone

Make Dinner Time Less Dreadful

- Choose a new recipe once per week to keep cooking exciting
- Allow yourself to make easy, quick meals or get take-out a couple of times per week if it's in the budget
- Watch a cooking show to be inspired. (I love Joanna Gains' Magnolia Table)

Teach Yourself a Handicraft

I've never been particularly good at these or have had the patience to even try, but getting over the hurdle of getting started can be rewarding and might be something you end up loving to do. Handicrafts are a good hobby for mothers because it is something to do while the kids are playing and you still want to be present.

- Embroidery
- Crocheting/knitting
- Sewing or weaving
- Felting kits
- Quilling
- Homemade cards for holidays or other occasions
- Air dry clay modeling and painting
- Diamond painting
- Home decor crafts

Find Joy in Making Something Out of Nothing

I remember a time when I was little and I complained that there wasn't anything to eat. My mom told me to go wait in the living room while she fixed something up. I wondered how she would do that because the cupboards were practically bare. A few minutes later she served me a plate that looked like a whole platter of different snacks. She called it a "surprise plate." All of the little things that I wouldn't have thought to eat suddenly looked delicious. I asked her how she did that and she said, "moms have a special way of making something out of nothing."

The Beauty of Books & Other Reading Materials

Books can do so many things for mothers. When I was a young, new mom who was feeling lonely and sad that I didn't really have a life outside of being a mom to a baby, I chose to pick up a book for the first time with the intent to read for fun. I was never a reader before then and never thought I would be. I got lucky on my first try and found a book that was interesting enough not to put down. From there, I fell in love with books and became aware of how much they can do for anyone's soul. Always have a:

- Non-fiction book on hand so you're learning something new or being inspired in some way
- Fiction book, just for fun
- Book to read aloud to your children a couple of times per week, or everyday if you prefer
- Book with lots of photos, such as cookbooks, home living, or hobby books
- Magazines that you actually love to take your time reading
- Homeschool book for parents, of course
- Audiobook for times when you are only able to listen or if you just don't enjoy reading print books very much

Mother's Ambiance

- Put on a podcast or an audiobook
- Make playlists for the different moods you're in
- Try listening to violin cover music of popular songs as background noise. (Trust me, it's good).

Make Your Surroundings Pretty

- When purchasing any small items for you or your home, if possible, choose the pretty ones over the basic ones. It may cost a little more, but it will be more satisfying to look at or use, which will make any money spent on it more worthwhile.
- Bring home a book from the library that has a beautiful cover and display it on an end table or wherever it can be seen. It's a free way to change up decor often.
- Print mini posters with inspiring quotes that are aesthetically pleasing. You can make them yourself or purchase downloads online. Hang them above your desk, on a cork board, or on the fridge.
- Make a room feel new again by moving things around, adding thrifted pieces, or crafting something yourself to use as decor.
- Thrift or junk pick some old small furniture, such as an accent table, and paint them to look like new. Better yet, use something you already own and give it a new life. (Tip: Chalk paint rarely requires sanding and hides imperfections well).

A New Era for Mothers

It often takes a mother's absence to realize that she wants to be more present. I think that is why so many mothers are suddenly seeking something different than what the norm has been in recent years. Instead of living a completely separate life from their children and having very little time with them, mothers are running back to a life that they were not taught but are trying hard to learn for themselves. Whether that means she chooses to work less, stay home completely, or just wants to be more intentional with the time she has when she is around, mothers are switching things up. If you ever wonder if this slow living thing with your children is making a significant difference in their lives, just observe how much they appreciate your presence. It is then, that you will already know the answer.

Chapter 3

Preserving Childhood

Childhood is disappearing. Have you noticed? Maybe you have observed the empty neighborhoods that used to be filled with kids playing street hockey, and now you are not even sure if any children live in these areas at all. Or it could be the lack of little hands knocking on the door, asking if your child can come out to play. Did you see the child when you were out at a restaurant who was glued to a tablet, completely ignoring the crayons and paper provided for them? Maybe your child attended school for a period of time, and it gave you a glimpse of how much things have changed. Recess, field trips, and class parties barely exist anymore. Social development and basic skills have been pushed aside by higher reading and arithmetic standards.

Between the changing times and the hustle and bustle of long school days, where does that leave the children of our society? It forces them to grow up faster in too many ways to count. It takes away curiosity they would've had about the natural world. It plagues them with the inability to enjoy the simplest of things. Many don't know how to make use of boredom or discover interests that they didn't know they had. If they do find what sparks their interest, it doesn't matter because there is likely not enough time in the day anyways.

Slowing Down Childhood

When I first decided to homeschool eleven years ago, I hadn't yet realized the impact it would have on my children's lives. I knew in my heart that there would be educational gains by going this route, but I asked myself if I might be somehow ruining their future. Would they turn out to be weird or different from other kids? That was the question that replayed in my mind.

As I reflected back on my own childhood, I remembered always feeling the pressure to fit in. If I did or said one thing wrong, it could potentially lead to other kids thinking I was uncool. My peers and I were always in such a hurry to grow up. Boys, clothes, and gossip were the main topics of discussion at lunchtime starting probably in third grade. I didn't really have any hobbies or talents. If I became interested in something, I had no idea how to pursue it. Mostly, though, I didn't know about many activities that existed. This left me feeling very bored after school unless my neighborhood friends were free to hang out. I became dependent on others to entertain me and make me feel less lonely. When I entered middle school, everything became increasingly more difficult. My grades stayed afloat for a while until I became behind in certain subjects because I couldn't keep up. There seemed to be a new math lesson every day when I was still catching on to what we were taught the week before. If a day of school was missed, the amount of make-up work was often worse than whatever sickness I had. Eventually, school became overwhelming and I stopped putting in much effort. When bullying became a severe issue, my mom finally decided that homeschooling was the best choice. I went on to graduate high school at seventeen, got a head start on college, then graduated with both honors and a lifelong friend that I met along the way.

Although the outcome of my life has been great, those memories from when I was a child made it occur to me that

I didn't want the same path for my own kids. I decided that I would slow down their childhood. Academics would be filled with curiosity, wonder, and real learning. Together, we would find what sparks their interests. I would also give them enough free time each day to carry out those activities. Making plans for homeschool outings or mini adventures together were important too, but I wanted to be careful not to over schedule either. Socialization would come from smaller groups compared to a school environment. This resulted in close to zero occurrences of bullying and increased conversations and friend making among the group of kids. I kept my children out of homeschool cooperatives (co-ops) that were mainly based around academics and enrolled them into co-ops where the sole purpose was to learn interesting things, make stuff, spend time outside, and meet friends.

In the beginning, I had no idea what slow or simple living was, but I've been steadily embracing the lifestyle for years. One of my three kids will be graduating soon. My love for the slow life has rubbed off on her so heavily that she has outdone her mom. Aside from working at her part-time job and also volunteering at a local cafe by organizing books on their displays, she spends her days waking when she wants to, reading in a cozy nook for hours, completing her studies, partaking in self-directed learning, and making crafts. She is happy with the simple pleasures of life, is rarely bored or lonely, and lives at her own pace. I often watch her in amazement, thinking about the lovely life she is creating for herself as a result of the foundation she has been given.

Play is Important Work

I think that play is often thought of as something that should happen after work is completed. But for children, play is absolutely valuable "work." Not only do kids learn much faster through play, but it also gives them more time to enjoy childhood, which so many children do not have enough of. Adults also might make the mistake of thinking that play is mostly for younger children. In reality, older children will play in many ways if they are intrigued enough. Children are constantly being encouraged by external influences to grow up faster. As a result, traditional play seems to be ending sooner in a child's life. It's almost like childhood is evolving into something completely different. I am not comfortable with that. Are you?

Screen-Time as Free Time

When one of my sons was two years old, a tablet targeted at young children had became a popular new "toy" to purchase for children at Christmas time. A relative asked if she could buy one for him as a gift. I suggested that it wasn't a wise idea as he was pretty careless with regular toys already, not to mention he threw them down when he would get frustrated. She ended up buying one anyway and kept it at her house for him to use. This was during a time when screen addiction for young children was not a topic yet, and child researchers were probably more worried about how many hours of television time they were having. My son enjoyed the tablet, and for once, he was sitting down focusing on something for long periods of time instead of running wild through the house. As a young naive mom, I thought that had to be beneficial, right? I couldn't have been more wrong.

As my son matured and the world pushed electronics onto kids more and more, he became highly skilled with technology. Everyone knew it was his special niche. I thought it was nice that he had something he was

good at and was also learning many things in the process,

such as coding, programming, and how a computer worked.

Eventually though, he didn't have any interest in being a kid

anymore. He would isolate himself unless I forced him to

come out of his room. When I put limits on screens, he

would become depressed, anxious, and moody. He did not

know how to play anymore. In fact, he had no desire to

engage in it whatsoever. New toys were tossed into his closet

to be forgotten about. His social skills declined and he was

diagnosed with high functioning autism. We thought that

the reason why he was so obsessed with electronics was

because it was an autistic trait and technology was just his

special thing.

Last year, I read up on multiple sources about screen

addiction in children and the side-effects that result from it.

These effects sounded spot on when comparing them with

my child's behaviors. We decided to take the leap and do a

screen detox for a few weeks. The plan was to take away all

screens except for television, but video apps weren't allowed.

After the detox, I would give the screens back, but with

limited use. As one could expect, my son was devastated and he put up a fight. For the two weeks, I made sure to make plans that would keep him occupied. Overnight stays at Grandma's, bowling, the mall, movie nights at home, and a lot of board games helped to keep his mind off of what he was going through. I may have even gone overboard and bought him a pet hamster to give him something new in his life.

By the end of the three weeks, we were already seeing a kid that we didn't recognize...a 12-year-old boy who was learning how to keep himself occupied, wanted to be around people again, and was discovering what else sparked his interest besides technology. Following the success of the screen fast, I really didn't want to give him electronics back at all, but we live in a digital age, his peers play video games, and I didn't want to take away something he was good at. So we put a three-hour limit per day of non-TV screen use. I understand it sounds like a lot still, but for him, it has been the perfect balance. He rarely complains when it's time to turn off his devices, I don't hear him constantly complaining of boredom, and I feel like I have my boy back.

Most children in America now spend five to seven hours per day in front of a screen (MedlinePlus Medical Encyclopedia, 2023). Screens are everywhere these days, including inside classrooms. Parents are the most important source to counteract the effects of screen use. Create a childhood where your kids know the importance of balance, and where they are not dependent on screens.

You're Never too Old to Play Outside

The outdoor world is a child's natural playground, yet sadly it is often disregarded among today's youth. Being in nature nourishes the slow living lifestyle by making individuals appreciate the vast world around them. For children, gaining an admiration for the outdoors doesn't mean sitting quietly in nature while listening to birds. Adults may be pleased with doing so, but children most likely will not be intrigued to spend time outside if that's what the expectation is.

Toddlers and other young children are curious beings. They normally love to touch and feel everything new. Sticks, rocks, and mud fascinate them. Letting them get dirty and *really* play when they have the opportunity to do so is important. Admittedly, I used to hate when my kids would get dirty. I preferred their clothes stayed decent looking and to not have to put them into the bath tub as soon as we came back inside from playing. I had a rushed mindset back then, not wanting anything "slowing" me down because I had too many other things to do. Little did I realize that's what we needed the most. As a way to break my old habits, I now remind myself that a little bit of dirt doesn't hurt. I set aside old clothes that are meant to be played in, toys that I'm okay with being filled with dirt, and even have a designated area in my backyard where my youngest is allowed to dig as much as he wants.

As children grow, their interests change. They don't just want to explore the objects in front of them, but they want to discover what else there is to see. This is a good time to find new walking trails, parks, beaches, creeks, or interesting land features. Old-fashioned play is still a part of a child's life at this time. Building sand castles, forts, or model boats to put in the water may be of interest. Riding their bike, flying kites, or roller skating may be too. I think this is also the time period when children start to consume too much technology and indoor activities that are available to them, which result in less of a desire to go outside. Don't let these external factors get in the way of a child's love for being outdoors. It's important now then ever to lead them into the right direction.

When children turn into preteens/teenagers, their interests take a dramatic turn. Don't be mistaken, though, older kids play outside too, just differently. It might look like playing basketball with friends, riding bikes through a local trail, disc golf at the park, reading a book on the deck, or fishing with their grandpa. If you have a child in this age range, you may notice sometimes that they easily get in a rut of wanting to stay indoors for a long period of time. Instead of telling them to go outside and find something to do, invite them to do something with you. Another way to motivate your teen to get outside is to create a meetup with another kid or group of kids close to their age. I recently created a small flag football event for some local homeschool teens at a park. It only cost fifteen dollars for supplies and took ten minutes to make an event page on social media. Each teen showed up excited to play in the park that day. No matter how old they get, they are never too old to play outside.

The Lost Art of Creativity

Everyone is born with the urge to channel their inner artist, but for many, creativity whithers away as they age. As an adult, can you recall times when you have gotten excited about using your creativity? Maybe when you decorated your child's cake, put together a project for your homeschool co-op, redecorated a room, made a wreath, or came up with a landscape design for your yard? The act of creating brings out interests and passions in people, no matter how young or old. The problem is that as children age, their freedom to explore their creativity lessens because the opportunities do not present themselves as often. Including more activities that will inspire kids to use their imagination, problem-solving skills, and innovativeness will help to uncover talents, spark interests, and find joy in the current moment.

Very Young Children (0 to 5)

Oftentimes, the toys parents give their children may not be used in the way they were intended. Their imaginations run wild, and they like to pretend an object is something completely different. They also love to mix up their toys and play with different objects that don't go together, despite parents wanting to keep everything organized. These are ways young children use their creativity. To help harness their abilities, parents can try some of the examples below.

- Provide plain paper as opposed to coloring books.
- Allow modeling clay to be mixed up.
- Set up sensory bins, changing out themes often.
- Use open-ended toys, such as blocks or a stacking rainbow.
- Make time to get messy, such as painting or cookie decorating.
- Expose them to various genres of music and play with instruments.
- Set up dramatic play areas, such as a pretend post office or farmers market.
- Play dress up.

Elementary & Pre-teens (6 to 12)

For a typical child at this age, the opportunity to create is usually cut down drastically. Pencil and paper for most school subjects, a busy schedule, and too many video games can disrupt valuable time. It is also often mistaken that children in this particular age range have outgrown certain types of toys, playing, and creating. Parents might put toys away or get rid of them when they think their child is too old for them. They may also stop setting up activities that they think only a younger child would enjoy. My twelve-year-old will not play with anything else if a video game is offered as an option. When they are not an option, I will find him fiddling with marble run kits or building with building bricks that have been stashed away in his closet. Electronics can be used for creative endeavors too. My son enjoys coding and making games for his virtual reality headset more than actually playing on it.

- Supply materials that will invite them to make things, such as building bricks, watercolors, or diamond art.
- Make a tinker box. Include items that they can fiddle, experiment, and invent with. Old wires, cardboard tubes, popsicle sticks, and etc..
- Use simple handicrafts or model building kits.
- Reverse engineer old electronics.
- Try Coding or digital art.
- Provide various art supplies to experiment with.

Teenagers (13 to 17)

Teens are at a fun age, despite what many may think. Getting creative really gives them a chance to see what they are passionate about. It can also give them productive hobbies to promote positive mental health and fill time when they are bored or lonely. My daughter has had so much time on her hands while being homeschooled her whole life, which has given her an immense amount of freedom to discover what she likes. I'll often open up her bedroom door to find her working on a new project. Being older has also opened up doors for what she can do with her projects. Posting art on to social media or videos of projects in the making are other ways to express creativity.

- Blog writing
- Digital art
- Advanced coding programs
- Competing in contests related to a creative interest
- Blacksmithing
- Soap or candle making
- Film making or photography
- DIY accessories or jewelry
- Cooking or cake decorating
- Book binding
- Self-publishing books
- Gourmet coffee making
- Wood carving

Influencers

The people that children spend time around can make, bend, or break their childhood. Of course our kids need to experience all different walks of life to be prepared for the world, but filling their lives with individuals who have a positive impact will hopefully steer them in the right direction.

Our society has become so used to the fact that students are bullied in school on a regular basis that they think trauma resulted from it is necessary for their well-being. The truth is, though, a lot of kids are suffering on a daily basis and many of them do not have the mental capability to handle it. Adults just see kids being immature kids and have the wisdom to know that what those children say or do towards others is complete nonsense. We also know that they will grow out of that kind of bullying. But to children, that is their whole world. They are not thinking about the future and how some day they will grow up and not be bullied in the same way that they currently are. That kind of thing can make children very depressed, anxious, or have a poor self-image. I urge parents to not be afraid to pull their children from those situations if they do not improve. Whether kids attend school, a hybrid program, extracurriculars, or a homeschool cooperative, continuous bullying can occur anywhere, and they should never have to endure that. Bullying can significantly affect their childhood.

You have probably heard the phrase "you are who your friends are." A decent kid can lose their way if they hang around the wrong crowd. The scary thing is that it only takes one individual to make that happen, not a whole group. Even so, we want our kids to pick and choose their friends, navigating their social lives for themselves so they can learn from mistakes, see people for who they really are, and so on. They may also learn more about the world through their friends when it comes to certain topics that parents might not necessarily approve of them knowing yet. This is all a part of growing up. However, if a parent finds that a specific friend or group of friends are influencing their child to grow up *too* fast, in a way that they don't think is healthy, they shouldn't be afraid to separate them if needed. After all, that is part of a parent's job.

Good influences can come from many places besides a child's direct family. Peers, instructors, family friends, or other individuals in your community can be role models that catapult an impressionable kid onto a decent path. Even though there will always be negative influences in a child's life, if the good ones drastically outweigh the bad ones, it's more likely that they will lead by the right example. You'll know when good people are hanging around your kid because they will influence them to mature in a way that does not take them away from their childhood too soon, or in a way that makes you feel uneasy.

Your children invite you to
slow down with them
everyday. It sounds like:
Can you play?
Can I help?
Can we do it together?
Accept the invitation as often as you can.

Chapter 4

Morning Time

Every day, mothers are tirelessly pushing through their busy mornings while children are hurrying to catch the bus, sometimes when it's still dark outside. After living that life for a few years, I saw the appeal of a homeschool morning time. This time of day represents togetherness as opposed to separation. It also provides children with a gentle awakening and eases them into their schedule for the day. Mothers can take advantage of the homeschool lifestyle by making mornings a time of contentment.

There have been different seasons of my life when I had to work, attend college, or fulfill many other obligations. If that meant that I couldn't be home with my kids at all hours, I put in a lot of effort to make sure they could still have a slow morning and a joyful childhood, even if that meant spending certain days with their grandparents. Everyone's life is different though. Some mothers are busier than others and some don't have relatives to depend on while they are working. No matter what your personal situation may be, don't get discouraged if every morning can't have a peaceful awakening or be time spent together. Do the best with what you have, when you can.

Weather, Calendar, & Seasons

Despite what some may think, making time for studying the weather, calendar, or four seasons are beneficial to children at all ages, not just young ones. Although the methods used can vary from age to age, there is still a lot to be learned whether they are three or thirteen.

The four seasons can be something to embrace with children. Decorating your homeschool area for the current season, preparing crafts or art projects, or setting out seasonal themed breakfast foods are cozy ideas if wanting to use the seasons as a theme. Since nature is the center focus of this area, you could study the changing seasons and how it effects nature as well. Nature journaling, documentaries, or viewing items found outside under a microscope are just a few ideas. This specific topic is discussed more in-depth in the nature study chapter.

The weather is usually still a brand new topic for preschoolers and kindergarteners. Talk about what it currently looks like outside, such as if

Rainbow sensory table

it is rainy, snowy, or foggy. They love discussing rainbows, how clouds move, and where rain comes from. Using a weather wheel, a weather chart, or some other tangible resource that kids can manipulate will be the most engaging. Reading books, both non-fiction and fiction, can help explain to them better about the types of weather that exist and why. Making crafts can also reinforce the ideas they have learned.

As children get older, they are able to dive deeper into how weather affects the world.

Rainbow light catcher

Observing the temperature each day and recording it on a chart or in a weather journal is a good place to start. You can also encourage them to make predictions, study the clouds, wind speed, and precipitation accumulation. Learning about weather doesn't have to stop at a certain age. Teenagers can get more hands-on with their weather observations too, such as making real-life rain collectors in their backyard. Another resource is interactive meteorology trainings or courses that can be found online.

Let's talk about calendar time. For littles, setting up a station for this with a display of each day of the month is what they need to really visualize the days ahead and understand what tomorrow means. Repetition when studying the days of the week and months of the year will lay the solid foundation. Then, when ready, they'll remember how many days are in each month, the holidays and seasons that correlate with each one, and how far away a future event is.

Should calendar time be just for young children? Absolutely not, it just looks a lot different for older kids and teens. Being homeschooled sometimes means that they might not write down the date every single day like they do in school when putting it at the top of their worksheets. Children should be encouraged to use a planner every morning. They can check what the current date is, what activities are coming up, and even what their assignments are for the day or when they are due. Setting aside time to take a look at their planner each day will help with time management skills and instill a sense of responsibility when it comes to deadlines or other events to prepare for.

Current Interests

Using current interests for morning time is the perfect way to increase the chances that your child will be excited to start their day and can promote a love for learning. Choose an interest that they have, check out books from the library, print relatable worksheets, and prepare simple activities ahead of time. You could pull up related videos and have discussion questions on hand to talk about or if they are old enough, let them research their interests on their own. For younger children, making a sensory bin or dramatic play area based on the chosen interest are other ideas.

Some interest-led themes that I have used in the past include farm animals, embroidery, tinker time, construction,  the Titanic, mythology, Woodstock, cardboard engineering, and soldering electronics. Some might think that certain topics are not educational enough because they are not traditional school topics, but if children are learning something new, then why not?

Soldering activity

Homeschooling Through the Holidays

Before I started homeschooling, I didn't realize how much there was to learn about holidays, in addition to celebrating them. From the history and different cultural traditions, to the passion that individuals have for certain holidays, there are endless lessons that can be learned by all ages. My favorite part about incorporating holiday studies into our homeschool is the coziness that it brings.

Some homeschool moms like to include their own religious celebrations and beliefs when teaching about certain holidays, such as Christmas or Easter. Others like to keep holiday studies secular, and many will use the opportunity to explore and learn about other people's religious holidays. You can choose whatever floats your boat. I created a list of homeschool activities on the next page that are related to different holidays and included a variety of things to do and learn.

Valentine's Day morning preparations.

New Years Eve/Day

- Make a vision board
- Write a pretend newspaper with the child's past year in review
- Write an essay about the most interesting thing that has happened in the past year
- Set a book list goal

Martin Luther King Day & Black History Month

- Watch a movie that is age appropriate. My favorites are:
1. My Friend Martin
2. The Color of Friendship
3. Ruby Bridges
4. Hidden Figures
- Write your own "I Have a Dream" speech
- Listen to the "I Have a Dream" speech and discuss what made the speech moving or well written
- Learn about African American inventors
- Biography studies
- Make a diversity sensory bin using different shades of beans to start a conversation about diversity with little ones
- Recreate famous African American works of art
- Learn about the history of jazz
- Do a Kente cloth paper weaving craft

President's Day & Election Week
- Build Lincoln's log cabin with popsicle sticks and glue
- Write an "if I were president speech"
- Learn about national symbols and monuments
- Biography studies
- Set up a pretend voting area equipped with ballots, a ballot box, registration cards, and an "I voted" badge
- Learn the differences between the presidential parties and discuss which one you and your children would like to choose or not choose
- Watch a presidential debate
- Have each child choose a president to research and present their findings at the end of morning time

Easter
- Learn about the history of Easter
- Do a Peter Rabbit book study
- Make crosses with sticks and twine
- Make Mexican Easter eggs with confetti
- Watch videos about the Easter story (there are Christian and non-Christian perspectives)
- Make decorations for your home or learning area
- Prepare a week long study, starting with Palm Sunday and the days leading up to Easter Sunday
- Complete a rabbit unit study

Stick & twine cross.

Read Across America, Mother Goose, Library Worker's Day

- Fill brown paper bags with random items. Each child chooses a bag without knowing what's inside then makes up a story based on the items.
- Dr. Seuss books and crafts
- Dr. Seuss biography
- Make bookmarks
- Make and give a small gift to your favorite librarian or all librarians working in the children's section
- Read books & complete unit studies for different Mother Goose rhymes
- Set up dramatic play areas based on Mother Goose ryhmes
- Learn the skill of bookbinding

Veterans & Independence Day

- Write letters to veterans or soldiers who are actively in the military or overseas
- Read about how the Star Spangled Banner came to be America's national anthem
- Learn how the American flag got its design
- Memorize the lyrics to *America the Beautiful* or *This Land is Your Land*
- Together, write a constitution for your family

Halloween

- Research the history of Halloween
- Listen to audio recordings of short scary stories while coloring or drawing Halloween pictures
- Do a study of Edgar Allen Poe and his writing
- Play the Clue or Clue Jr. boardgames
- Assign mystery story writing prompts

All Soul's Day Pastries

A holiday created by Roman Catholics that has been almost completely forgotten and was celebrated after Halloween was known as All Soul's Day. This day was believed to be a day when dead loved ones would be cleansed of their sins in preparation to be released from Purgatory and enter Heaven. People would use this day to remember those specific loved ones who they thought might be stuck in Purgatory (a place between Heaven and Hell). On All Soul's Day, people would bake pastry-like cakes made from fruits, flour, and spices, and then hand them out when a begger would come to their door. In return, the beggers would be expected to pray for the dead loved ones of that household.

Directions

1. Pre-heat oven to 375 F.
2. Mix sugar and butter together, then mix in the eggs.
3. In a separate bowl, mix flour and spice together, then add into the first bowl.
4. Stir in the raisins.
5. Add a little milk until the dough softens.
6. Flatten the dough with a roller, making it a quarter of an inch thick.
7. Cut out the cakes with round or square cookie cutters.
8. Make criss-cross mark on the tops.
9. Place them on a greased cookie sheet and bake for 10 minutes or until golden brown.

Ingredients

- 6 oz butter
- 6 oz caster sugar
- 3 egg yolks
- 1 lb. flour
- 2 teaspoons of mixed spices (pumpkin, apple pie or, cinnamon, or nutmeg are good choices)
- 4 oz raisins
- a little milk as needed

Thanksgiving

- Look up the "Mayflower Society" online. This group of Mayflower descendants educates others about the role of the Pilgrims in history. They run the Mayflower Society House, a museum in Plymouth, Massachusetts.
- The Native American dice game can be found online.
- Make a gratitude tree. Fill a vase with sticks, then cut out orange, red, and yellow paper into leaf-shaped pieces. Use a hole puncher to make holes on the leaves and loop ribbon through each one. Everyone writes different things they are thankful for on a leaf, then hang them on the tree.

Make Corn Husk Dolls

Corn husk dolls are a fun old-fashioned craft that is also a toy.

Directions
1. Soak four husks in water for ten minutes, then pat dry with a paper towel.
2. Place them in a stack.
3. About an inch from the top, tie husks together with twine.
4. Flip upside down, then fold pieces over so that it covers the twine.
5. Add another piece of twine to form a head.
6. Roll one husk and place a tie at each end. This will be the arms.
7. Stick the arm piece through the body to secure them in place.
8. Tie another piece of twine in the middle to form a waist.

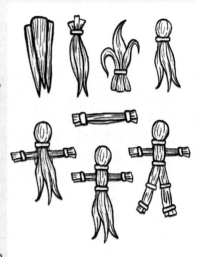

Christmas

- Make a Christmas village sensory bin using plastic village pieces.
- Prepare an advent of your choice. You could do a holiday-themed activity each morning such as reading a different book each day. If religious, you could study the Christmas story and baby Jesus for the month of December.
- Make or write inside of cards and pass them out at a nursing home.
- Learn about the story of St. Nicholas.
- Set up a Christmas around the world week where your children learn about a different country's holiday traditions each morning.

Tree Party for the Birds

Give the birds in your backyard a a present by decorating a tree with edible ornaments.

Directions

1. Choose a birdseed blend for the kinds of birds in your yard.
2. Choose oranges or apples as the base.
- Oranges: cut in halves and hollow out. Pierce two holes with a tooth pick to thread twine through, knotting to stay in place. Then fill with seeds.
- Apples: slice into rings, spread peanut butter all over them, then press seeds against them until they stick. Pierce one hole through the apple with a toothpick for twine.

Homemade bird feeders.

Morning Invitations

Morning invitations are gifts of learning that are designed with intention. Invitations are play or creativity-based activities that are also open-ended, meaning the child can decide what to do with the invitation and let their imagination run wild. It starts with an idea or theme, then the gathering of supplies, and lastly, the setting up.

My youngest son loves entering our homeschool room to unexpectedly find an invitation. Sometimes, I'll use his sensory bins, and other times I'll display a new activity on his shelf or desk. For my older children, a basket filled with stuff or an activity on our dining room table may be waiting for them. The invitation can be a very simple activity, such as a building challenge with printed task cards or a felt craft. It can also be something that takes a little more prep work, such as constructing a dramatic play theme. Morning invitations do not have to happen every single day. You could even choose to do one per week or leave something out that can be used all week long. Don't let yourself become burnt out over planning these activities. Think of them as little sprinkles of fun added into your child's week.

Invitation Themes

- Crafts or art
- Building or engineering
- Animal habitats, such as forests or oceans
- Geography & cultures
- Farming, harvesting, & preserving
- Gardening, flower drying, & flower pressing
- Fairytales
- Book-related
- Nature-based, such as bugs or tree identification
- Investigation, mysteries, or escape room challenges
- History-related, such as the Vikings, Civil War, or mummies
- Science, such as observations, experiments, space, dinosaurs, & simple machines
- Community helpers & careers
- Modeling clay kits
- Construction, vehicles, & planes
- Camping, survival skills, hunting, & fishing
- Mythology, folklore, & urban legends
- Reverse engineering
- "Create your own" task, such as "create your own jungle" with loose parts, or "create your own castle" with blocks

The possibilities are endless!

Invitation Supplies

- Dyed rice, sand, or dried beans for sensory table
- Sticks, rocks, artificial moss & leaves, pine cones, acorns, wood slices, bark, shells, & seeds
- Paper, colored pencils, glue, duct tape, crayons, sketchbooks, mixed media paper, paint brushes, & paint
- Cardboard, cardstock, shoe boxes, & popsicle sticks
- Beads, pipe cleaners, glitter, felt, pom poms & stickers, fabric, gems, yarn, & twine
- Blocks, magnet tiles, & building bricks
- Peg dolls
- Miniature items for small world play
- Modeling clay
- Lids, CDs, straws, paper towel tubes, keys, rubber bands, coffee cans, & filters
- Gears, keyboard keys, wire, magnets, wheels, nuts, & bolts
- Old puzzle pieces, game pieces, & marbles
- Wrapping paper, paper bags, tissue paper, & paint sample cards

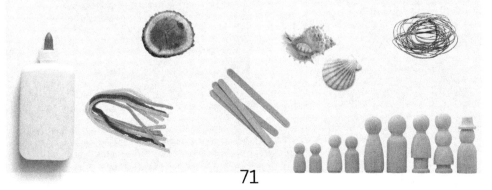

Chapter 5

Reading & Literature

Pre-reading Skills

There's been much debate about whether to teach children the letter sounds or the letter names first. I decided to use the sound approach when I taught my youngest how to read because when letters are completely new to a child, the names can interfere with memorizing the sounds. The sounds of letters are ultimately what a child needs to master in order to begin the process of learning to read. Also, what many people do not realize is that if a child struggles with reading down the road, or it is discovered that the child has dyslexia, using this method can make a drastic difference in their reading success. Some like to teach vowels first, then consonants, while others start at the beginning of the alphabet until reaching the end. I personally went in the order from A to Z and saw results decently fast, so I don't see anything wrong with that method. When teaching vowels though, you'll only teach short sounds at this stage.

When teaching letter sounds, start with uppercase letters only, as this will keep it uncomplicated. You could purchase a reading curriculum, but it is not necessary for this initial step.

Letter Sound Activities

Where to Start

You'll start by teaching only one letter sound. After a lot of practice, you'll keep reviewing that initial sound while adding a second, but practice them separately. For example, spend a few minutes practicing the old sound, then another few minutes on the new one. Once you think your child has had a lot of practice, you'll set up activities where the two sounds are compared, such as sorting matching objects to their corresponding sound. Once your child has mastered both sounds, you will do mini review sessions four to five days per week of all mastered sounds. You don't want to spend too long doing this because it will become repetitive and they will feel bored. You'll spend an additional few minutes on a fun activity that teaches a new sound that they are working on.

Gather objects that begin with the letter. Say to your child, "These objects make the 'ah' sound." (Letter a). Pull one out at a time, saying the name of them clearly. Have your child repeat what you did.

Use printables. Point to each object, saying it aloud. Ask your child if it makes the same sound as the letter you're working on. They can also circle them if they are able to.

Write the letter down multiple times and draw dots underneath. Roll modeling clay into balls and place them on each dot. As your child says the sound, squash the clay with their hands.

Mixing Up Sounds

To ensure complete mastery of a letter sound, your child will have to be able to correctly identify them when they are amongst multiple other sounds. Some activities to try are below.

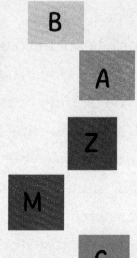

Gather objects that begin with different letters. Ask your child to pull one out that makes a certain sound. Keep repeating until the basket is empty.

Use toy cars to run over letters while saying the sounds.

Cut out multiple colors of paper, write a different letter on each one, and make a path on the floor with them. Have your child step on each one, saying the sounds as they go.

Make a sensory bin with dyed rice, uncooked noodles, or sand. Hide magnetic letters inside. Have your child scoop each one out while saying their sounds.

Print clothespin activities where your child has to clip the clothespin onto the correct picture that matches the sound.

Teach the Alphabet

After the letter sounds are mastered, teaching the letter names are next, along with upper and lowercase letters. Practicing at least four days per week for ten to fifteen minutes should be sufficient enough. At this stage, pencil and paper writing is not yet encouraged as that is a separate skill. Instead, children should work their way up to writing by using a multisensory approach to letter recognition. This includes activities such as filling in a letter with paint on an activity sheet, making letter crafts, or attempting to draw letters in the sand.

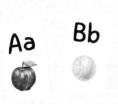

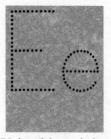

Pick only one word to associate with each letter of the alphabet until your child has mastered the sounds and corresponding letters. For example, practice saying "a for apple and b for ball" repeatedly. This word will give your child something to reference back to when they are trying to think of the letter name and what sound each one makes.

Using bingo ink or a Q-tip and paint, have your child dot an outline of the letters. This builds memory of the letter shapes and is a pre-writing skill.

Making letter themes is a fun addition to practicing letter names and what they look like.

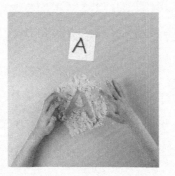

Have your child use their finger or a stick to draw letters in sand. This builds memory of the letter shapes and is also a pre-writing skill.

Choose a Reading Curriculum

Once the alphabet and sounds are mastered, then your child will be ready for a reading curriculum. Some might not use an actual curriculum, but I find that it's the most thorough way to make sure that no steps are missed, and it takes the burden off to know that you have an organized plan. If you think your child is ready to start the next step, remember that every child is different and the pace at which they learn to read will look different too. Take your time to teach them. Slow and steady is what's important.

My Favorite Curricula for Teaching Children How to Read

The Good & the Beautiful **Language Arts**

This company offers a preschool curriculum that teaches the pre-reading fundamentals and a kindergarten language arts set that takes your child all the way to where they need to be as far as reading goes. It's also a beautiful curriculum.

All About Reading by *All About Learning Press*

This company uses a multisensory approach and is extremely thorough. This would also be a good curriculum if your child is struggling or is suspected of having dyslexia.

Instill a Love of Reading

As a child, I was never much of a reader. Looking back, I think I came close to being one, but my love of reading was hindered throughout childhood. Once I finally discovered that I did in fact like books, I was in my late teen years. I thought to myself how I missed out on another world for all of those years.

When I was five years old, my dad brought home audiobooks on cassette tapes that he had gotten from someone. I quietly lay on my bed listening to The Ugly Duckling and other classics from my boom box. I never fast-forwarded through any of them. I took in every word. It amazed me how I could listen to a story that easily, even though I didn't know how to read yet. After those stories got old, I never listened to an audiobook again. That was because no one brought home any more and this was before everything was so easily accessible on the internet. So that was the end of that.

I remember sitting on my bedroom floor looking at picture books, making up stories as I went along because, again, I couldn't read yet. There were times when my mom used to read books to me, which I loved. Unfortunately, my mom was busy working a lot, so it didn't happen too often. Once I started figuring out how to read, I was over the moon and had my own little shelf with books that I'd look at and attempt to read sometimes.

As I got older, my mom took me to the library for my very own library card. I was finally ready for chapter books, and I remember feeling like it was an exciting day. I had never been to the local library before, and I was in awe of the endless books to be read. I had recently watched the movie Matilda and thought it was cool that she would check out so many books from the library and read every single one of them. The reality though? Chapter books took a lot more mental effort to finish reading than picture books did. I had many things on my mind... like going outside, watching TV, and playing with toys. Sadly, I missed out on not only many great books, but a hobby I could've loved.

In school, we were made to read. That might have been my chance to realize how nice it was to read a book from start to finish, but I never liked the books that were chosen for me. Therefore, I hated books, or so I thought I did.

Instilling a love of reading increases stronger spelling, comprehension, vocabulary, and writing skills, which affects all parts of a child's education. My favorite result though is that it expands a child's perspective on so many topics that they may otherwise never would've experienced firsthand. Not everyone will love to read books, but I believe that many would if reading was fostered the right way throughout a person's childhood.

When a child is young, they should be read to on a regular basis, even if they are too rambunctious to sit still. If this is the case, read to them when they're playing in the bath tub or while they are eating lunch. Audiobooks can also be used no matter the age. Put one on while your child is coloring, completing a puzzle, or even while doing school work that wouldn't be hindered by listening to a book.

Teaching children how to find a book that they'd like to read is a very important part of instilling a love of reading. Many years ago, one of my children received speech therapy from our local public school. The speech room was off of the school's library, so we'd walk through it to get there. On more than one occasion I was able to hear the way the

the librarian spoke to the children. From what I gathered, she had a rule about the books. If a student took a book off the shelves, then that would be the book they were stuck checking out. Apparently, she didn't have the confidence that they would put them back in the same exact spot, and she didn't want to deal with it even though that was her job. I'd expect that as a librarian, the other part of her job was to convince children to love books, which she was clearly failing to do also.

My daughter and I like to go to the bookstore often and grab a few books for each of us that look interesting. We sit in the cafe with our shakes and look through our own books. We have this rule that if we read the first couple of pages of a book and we are intrigued to read more, then that's the book we'll take home. It's easy to start a book, only to find that you are dreadfully bored early on. That's not going to make anyone enjoy reading, and they definitely are not going to care to finish the book. I have found that I am an extremely picky reader. That is probably why I thought I hated to read for many years of my childhood. The problem was that I just didn't know what I liked or how to go about finding one that I'd be motivated enough to finish.

When helping your child find a book for themselves, use the same rule where they must pick the book that still holds their interest after reading the first one or two pages. Only then would I recommend setting aside some time a few days per week where you expect them to read, unless they do so on their own. Be a reading role model by spending reading time together. Create a cozy atmosphere to make the time more appealing and that you can both look forward to. It can even be a group activity if more than one child wants to come and join in. Comfy chairs, a sunroom, or a spot on the patio on a nice day are some ideas. Special snacks or drinks are a good addition too.

Book Themes for Young Children

To make books more inviting to my children, I love to let my inner librarian come out and create themes for a specific book or topic. For example, if I chose a storybook about scarecrows during the autumn season, I'd set up a scarecrow craft, print a related worksheet, and add in some non-fiction information about crops and why scarecrows are used. I might even add in activities about crows.

In the past, I chose fairytales as a theme. I made some play-based activities including a "build your own castle" challenge out of blocks, added fairytale finger puppets I found at the dollar store, and made a homemade castle from a cardboard box.

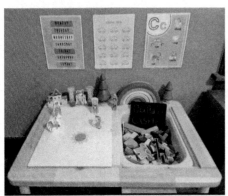 

"Build a castle" challenge   Cardboard box castle

This kind of story experience takes a child beyond the pages of a book and immerses them in its world. It allows children the ability to examine the characters, setting, and plot much more closely than a simple reading comprehension worksheet would. I am a firm believer that if playing can be incorporated into learning, that should be taken advantage of. To be realistic, don't pressure yourself into feeling like you have to do extravagant activities for every book. The simplest activities can still be inspiring.

Family Novel Studies

The purpose of a family-style novel study is to take your children on a reading adventure from beginning to end, helping them to see a book all the way through. In addition to improving comprehension, vocabulary, and fluency, novel studies are opportunities for mothers to create a cozy atmosphere that brings their family together while being entertained by a good book.

An error that is often made when choosing a novel to study is thinking that only classic books or books that are most commonly read should always be what is picked out. My oldest child is very much an avid reader. She is the type of teenager who spends most of her extra money on books and keeps a book log of everything she has read. She knows what she likes but often likes to explore different kinds of books, including some of the classics. Even while being a big reader and often wanting to broaden her horizons for book genres, she has found that more than half of the classics that she reads, she is too bored to finish. She often finishes them anyway though, just to say she did.

Imagine if a child who doesn't like reading very much in

the first place, if at all, is forced to get through a book that he or she thinks is dreadfully dull. Will that child change their mind about it just because many people consider it to be a masterpiece? Probably not. Instead, they may learn to dislike reading even more. From what I have gathered, it is the opinion of some that children should be exposed to certain "good literature" no matter what they are interested in, simply because they are thought to be good. I say that life is too short to read uninteresting books when we have a whole world of them to choose from.

Besides choosing a book to read for a novel study, activities should be chosen to go along with it. Starting off with some kind of exciting book kick-off activity is a good way to introduce a new book. This can be done with themed snacks or decorations and discussing the book before reading it. One idea to start a discussion is to watch a book trailer for the chosen novel. These videos can usually be found online. Another idea is to make predictions together about the book and see who was the most correct at the end.

Throughout reading the chosen novel, there are many opportunities for activities. Comprehension questions that you have either prepared yourself, or ones you have pulled off the internet are wise to do regularly. Talk to your children about the difference between real and fake reading. For example, reading quickly to get through a chapter without paying attention to what is really happening is just fake reading. If your children know that there will be comprehension questions at the end of each chapter, this will encourage more real reading. Part of comprehension is studying and knowing new vocabulary words. If you have read a chapter ahead of your child, you can pick out words to discuss beforehand, or save the discussion for afterwards and check to see what they comprehended on their own.

To keep reading fun, prepare activities that your child can enjoy throughout the process and at the end.

Novel Activities

- Act out scenes. Don't be afraid to be silly!
- Pick a setting and paint what you think it looks like.
- Complete character one-pagers, write a pretend letter to a character, or create a character "wanted poster."
- Write an alternate ending, draw a new cover, or watch the movie after finishing the book.
- Email the author with questions or write a review.

Poetry Tea Time

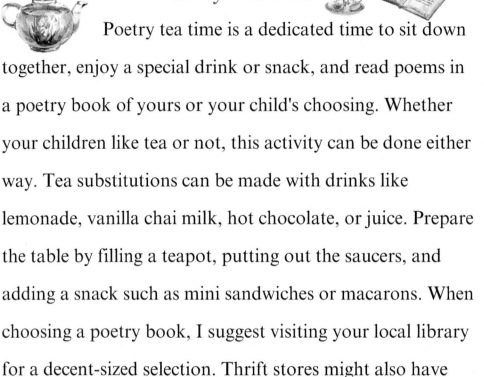

Poetry tea time is a dedicated time to sit down together, enjoy a special drink or snack, and read poems in a poetry book of yours or your child's choosing. Whether your children like tea or not, this activity can be done either way. Tea substitutions can be made with drinks like lemonade, vanilla chai milk, hot chocolate, or juice. Prepare the table by filling a teapot, putting out the saucers, and adding a snack such as mini sandwiches or macarons. When choosing a poetry book, I suggest visiting your local library for a decent-sized selection. Thrift stores might also have some poetry treasures. You may enjoy setting the scene yourself or encouraging your children to help you prepare for poetry tea time. Examples of how they can contribute are setting the table, prepping the food or drinks, choosing the poetry book options, and putting on some easy listening background music.

Reading poems out of a book randomly, from start to finish, or choosing your favorite ones then taking turns reading them aloud are different options. The most important focus of this activity is time spent together.

Reading Time for Mothers

If you want your children to love something, let them watch you participating in it as well. If they see you taking time for yourself to sit and read, they are more likely to model that behavior or even ask to join you.

Aside from inspiring your children to read, you should also inspire yourself. Whether you love to nourish your brain with non-fiction or fill your heart with fiction, reading books can reenergize your soul, making you a happier teacher, mother, and woman. So put a "mom" basket together with a couple of current reads, a magazine, a journal for your thoughts, and have it available to take anywhere. Another alternative is to set up a special spot in your home and romanticize the experience with goodies, your favorite mug, and soft lighting. My preferred spots are on my patio on a summer morning or in my cozy kitchen.

A mother's reading setup

89

Chapter 6

Writing, Spelling, & Grammar

Preparing to Write

Social media has allowed me to see into the lives of many mothers who are struggling to teach their children how to write. One thing that boggles my mind is when I read a post from a mother asking for help with teaching their two or three-year-old how to write. Young children need to do a lot of work before putting a writing utensil into their hands, such as digging, squishing, pulling, and grabbing. As children do this, they strengthen their fine motor skills. If you think that your child is capable of attempting to use a writing utensil but find that they are struggling, don't get frustrated. Instead, go back to the fine motor activities. Meeting them where they are will go a lot further than forcing something that isn't ready yet. To hold a pencil correctly, give them modeling clay and sensory bins.

Fine Motor Activities

Learning to Write

When a child is ready or eager to pick up a pencil, there are actually specific writing exercises to do before jumping into writing letters. The skill of drawing shapes, lines, and curves should be mastered first. This will pave the way to your child's writing abilities. Next, teach your child to write their name with a capital letter first and the rest done in lowercase letters. They'll start by tracing their name for a good while until they are ready to practice on their own. As they become more proficient with this, move on to capital letter practice the same way, tracing first, then writing them on their own. After your child has mastered capital and lowercase letters, continue to practice handwriting skills, as they will improve more and more over time. Copying sentences can come next while they are still learning to spell and write independently. They will also catch on to how punctuation works by copying sentences.

Slow & Meaningful Writing Practice

Teaching children how to be good writers must be done diligently. When I was a child, I often felt lost while being instructed to complete writing assignments. I knew that there was a basic structure to follow, such as  including an introduction, the details in the middle, and a conclusion. What I did not know was what words to actually use. The only introduction I knew for fiction was "once upon a time." The only introduction I knew for non-fiction was something like "I think" or "I'm going to tell you about..." As I sat at my desk trying to come up with the words, I remember wishing that the teacher would just tell me ideas for how to start an essay or story. I realize that the teacher probably thought that students should think of their own thoughts to write down, but maybe if I was ever given a list of examples, I would learn some effective ways to start an introduction and expand my writing abilities for the future.

Instead of thinking that children will learn to be good writers on their own eventually, what if we taught them from the get-go? The side-by-side writing method is when a parent sits next to their child while taking turns writing a sentence in a story or essay. The parent and child can also discuss different vocabulary words to use, such as when certain words are being overused or when wanting to improve the writing piece. The parent can show their child how easy it is to either use a thesaurus or the internet to find synonyms and antonyms of a word while writing. Together, the parent and child can craft the perfect introduction and conclusion, while the parent also teaches how to effectively transition from one paragraph to another in between.

Copy work is another method to use when teaching what good writing skills look like, but I think it's often not used to its advantage. It may be a common misconception that simply copying a paragraph from a good book or author will teach a child to write well on their own. Instead of blindly giving a child sentences to copy, have a specific skill in mind you want to work on with your child. For example, if your child struggles to understand what a conclusion should contain, then give them conclusive paragraphs to copy. Discuss with your child afterward the words that were used and why, along with how the original writer summarized their thoughts. If your child needs to learn the correct ways to use commas, then make that the focus. Copy work can be a powerful way to learn if it's done with care, and it will also be more meaningful in the end.

Creative Writing

Teaching children how to craft a creative writing piece should also be a creative process, not dry and boring. Children need to feel inspired if they are going to come up with interesting ideas and become excited to write about them.

One way to get the creative juices flowing is to write a story together with your child. Brainstorm and bounce ideas off each other. Next, decide on the plot, setting, and characters. Then, take turns writing sentences or paragraphs. Children will be able to see what the creative writing process looks like in a gentle way.

Retelling an already existing story can also be intriguing for children. They can choose a favorite book or recently read story, then put their own twist on it, kind of like a remake of a movie. Updating the original writing piece, changing the characters' personalities, writing a new ending, or switching it to a different setting are some things to experiment with.

When teaching creative writing, don't be afraid of untraditional methods. Children might enjoy putting together their own comic strip or even a graphic novel, especially if they like to draw and doodle. Another idea is to have your child create a mad lib for someone else to complete. If your child is interested in songwriting or screenplays, provide them with opportunities to explore those interests while enhancing their writing skills. Creative writing encompasses various avenues and can be seamlessly incorporated into a writing lesson.

Non-fiction Writing

Non-fiction writing is based on real events, facts, information, or people. It is true that this kind of writing prepares children for essays and research papers that will be required of them if they go off to college. Most of all though, it preps them for real-life tasks that they will face throughout their lives.

When a child is a new or young writer, starting them off with information they know is best. This can be done through daily journals by providing them with writing prompts about topics that they have experienced. Examples include writing about what they did over the weekend, something they are excited about, anything interesting they saw or did recently, or even thoughts that they have about a certain topic. This style of writing is called narrative writing because it's kind of like telling a story from the writer's point of view, except it's a true story.

As children become more experienced writers, they are able to move on to informative writing, which aims to inform the reader about a specific topic or issue. It might sound like a style only meant for older children, but kids are more ready for certain work than one may think. When I was in first grade, my teacher gave the class a writing prompt about landforms. We each had to choose any landform we wanted and then write a mini essay about it. I chose glaciers because at the time, I was obsessed with learning about the Titanic. After writing out my sentences with my mom's help and learning some pretty big vocabulary words to include in my essay, I had to present it to my class by reading it aloud. I surprisingly had a round of applause from my classmates because even they were not expecting me to enunciate some of the words I used, which was a huge confidence booster. If a child is able to choose informative topics that interest them whenever possible, they are far more likely to give you their best work. When a child reaches middle and high school, giving them proper research skills is necessary. This is also when you'll want to teach them about plagiarism and citing their references. Aside from learning these skills through a typical worksheet, pull out a non-fiction book and show them first-hand examples of how writers properly discuss topics in their own words while also including works of others. Show them the bibliography and reference pages in the back of the book and how they are used throughout the author's work.

When expressing one's opinion or stance on an issue, it is called persuasive writing. Every day, we are confronted with this kind of writing, whether it's on magazine covers, the internet, or billboards, or through spoken words such as a video, television, and radio. Even when the writer is simply sharing their opinion, they still have an agenda, and it involves persuading the reader to think the same way as the writer, or opening their mind to new thoughts or beliefs.

The skills that need to be obtained to effectively conduct this kind of writing involves learning how to convince or persuade the reader without simply telling them what they should do or think. The purpose is to evoke emotions, so that the reader will believe they are changing their opinions on their own. For young children, using phrases such as "I believe" at the beginning of their paper is fine to do, because that best suits their level of writing skills. However, key skills can be taught as young as third grade. Doing so will help children learn significant tips and tricks that will carry on throughout the rest of their education without wasting time on nonsense.

Get your child used to changing out phrases like "I believe" with phrases that get straight to the point. A writer can tell the reader what they think without actually telling you what they think. For example, instead of saying, "I think that we should save the penguins from going extinct because..," try saying, "Everyday, penguins are threatened with life or death. It's up to humans to do something about it." Using a compelling or startling hook such as that example did, will gain a reader's attention. The reader will also know what the writer's stance on an issue is without them directly saying it. When moving on throughout a persuasive essay, encourage your child to not only give supporting details about the issue, but to also look for opposing viewpoints and face them head-on by offering pros for why their stance is still the better choice.

When children come to realize that their written words give them power to have their voices heard, they look at writing in a different light. Writing well in multiple formats will come in handy for the rest of their lives, so don't rush through the process.

Snail Mail Monday

One of my favorite writing activities that gives a slow living feel is what I like to call "snail mail Monday." When Mondays come around, get out supplies to make a handwritten letter and then mail it to the chosen receiver. The activity lets your child practice how to compose sentences, work on handwriting skills, and double check for spelling and grammar mistakes. It also keeps an old-fashioned gesture alive and builds connections with others. When deciding who to send letters to, think of relatives, good friends, long distance family, community workers, personal role models, nursing home residents, or even public leaders. Writing letters to all different types of people gives the opportunity to learn about informal and formal writing and how to tune their words to fit the person they are writing to.

There is no need to limit your children to just the basic letter every week though. Cards, homemade bookmarks with quotes on them, postcards, and other paper crafts can be included as well. If you'd like to go a step further, a snail mail station or basket can be set up too. Be sure to include items like washi tape, stickers, fancy stationery paper, cardstock, ribbon, twine, scissors, stamps, and a variety of writing utensils. Giving your child their very own address book where they can record names and information of people to send letters to might also excite them.

When to Teach Spelling

For most children, reading comes much more easily than spelling. That is why it's usually recommended to teach a child the basics of reading before even thinking about teaching him/her how to spell. Reading actually prepares children to be successful spellers. As a child learns to read, they are practicing phonemic awareness skills such as rhyming and alliteration. A visual memory of many words is also being built in their minds that will help them spell those words later. Lastly, a child's hands are not all the way developed until age six or seven anyway. That doesn't mean that they cannot use a pencil at all until then, it just means that they should not be forced to use one for a long period of time. The act of reading is called "decoding." Successfully decoding words means the child is able to break words apart and figure out the sounds. This is the foundation for the next phase, which is "encoding," better known as putting letters together to spell words.

It is important to note that if a child seems to be ready for spelling, but they are consistently struggling through the process or easily forgetting words they already mastered, then learning disabilities such as dysgraphia or dyslexia should be considered before brushing things off as something they'll catch up on when they're ready to.

Teaching Methods for Spelling

Depending on your style of teaching, there are a few options to think about when deciding how to incorporate spelling practice into your child's day. If you prefer to be super organized without the extra stress of planning, then choosing a spelling curriculum would probably be best.

If you're not keen on past curricula you have tried, or just don't want to go that route, then you could take a spelling list from anywhere and use it as the spine of your teaching. For example, taking lists off the internet for your child's grade or taking one from an actual curriculum and then incorporating your own activities is what that would look like.

Another method is to pick and choose misspelled words from your child's mistakes when writing, then using those to study for a week or two. This would have to be utilized with older children since they need to be able to write a fair amount so that you have a place to gather words from.

Also, young children would benefit more from an organized approach that would guide them through the different spelling rules and patterns, such as memorizing word families. If your child is in middle or high school, though, and you are not formally teaching spelling anymore, this way of practicing spelling could be very beneficial. Aside from picking from their own misspelled words, using lists of the most commonly misspelled words is another great idea for this age group. A quick search online for your child's current grade level can provide those kinds of lists for you or a physical book of such words can also be purchased.

Lastly, if a lot of books are included in your homeschool, spelling words can be taken from the current book being read. Either look through a chapter while picking words for your child to study, or let them jot them down as they read independently if they are mature enough to take on the initiative to do so.

Teach Grammar Gently

Learning grammar doesn't have to feel like studying an electronic manual. When the subject is too technical and dry, that's how it might seem to children.

I can still remember sitting in my fourth-grade class completing an independent grammar lesson. I was supposed to take what I had learned the day before and show that I mastered the concepts. As I sat there struggling to get through the assignment, I asked myself how in the world was someone supposed to memorize each part of speech and why was it important anyway? The problem was that the lessons seemed to focus too much on mastering the terminology instead of teaching children how to use it to be effective communicators while writing.

When teaching your child the subject of grammar, try to limit the practice of memorization just for the sake of memorization. Put more energy into making connections to what the child reads and also how they write. If your child truly learns anything, then the definitions of terminology will likely follow afterwards, adding to their language arts skills.

Studying Grammar Through Literature

Make no mistake in thinking that grammar lessons must only come from a workbook. Real books give the child a chance to see grammar come alive through their favorite stories. Whether you choose a book as a novel study, a book that your child chose for independent reading, or you just pull a random book off the shelf, this method can be utilized for any of those situations.

Start by selecting a paragraph out of the reading material. It helps to have a specific skill in mind that you want your child to work on at that time, such as comma usage, punctuation, or capitalization of proper nouns. Be sure to find a paragraph that contains good examples for your lesson. Together, pick the paragraph apart. Discuss why the sentences are written the way they are. After going over that, encourage your child to write a sentence of their own that shows what they learned. If they get stumped, write an example for them first or write one together. Repeat these activities until your child has a firm grasp on the targeted skill before moving on. Keep in mind though that studying grammar will take many years before actually coming close to mastering it. The more it is practiced, the better the writer your child will become.

Practicing Good Grammar

Children should have first-hand experience editing for grammar mistakes before they can effectively write their own work without mistakes. Assign a paragraph with intentional grammar mistakes that your child has previously learned about. Also, tell them the number of grammar mistakes to look for. They can circle, underline, or add in marks to show what needs to be fixed. Once it is checked over by you, give your child the okay to rewrite the paragraph correctly. If your child cannot figure out some of the mistakes, provide them with the type of mistakes. For example, let them know that there are two punctuation mistakes, two capitalization mistakes, and one quotation mark mistake. In the occurrence that your child struggles with this activity, it's okay to give them the type of mistakes from the start until they improve.

Assessing Grammar Skills

Assessing a child's skills to check for understanding, mastery, or to discover weak areas should be completed at least once per week. This can be accomplished easily without a traditional test, but instead by applying real knowledge on the subject.

One way to evaluate your child's grammar is to read two to three sentences aloud while your child dictates what they hear. Start by reading the entire passage that you have selected so that your child can hear the whole message. Then repeat each sentence while they write it down in between. If your child does not do well with the auditory processing skills that it takes to complete such an assignment, then there is another way to go. Provide a written paragraph for your child to visually see, but without any grammar markings or capitalization. Also, do not give any clues as to what the paragraph needs. They will attempt to rewrite the paragraph on their own for their assessment.

Throughout your child's education, the grammar skills that they will have gained will naturally transfer over into their own work, making them wonderful writers.

Chapter 7

Mathematics

Math Doesn't Have to be Fast

Children can learn mathematics in two ways...through rote memorization or through multiple hands-on techniques. The difference? Rote memorization may seem quicker, but learning with the whole body goes deeper instead of just scratching the surface of a child's mind. With there being a vast amount of math concepts to learn throughout a child's education, it may seem intriguing to work through each one quickly in fear of easily becoming behind. The thing is though, if a child can't spend a decent amount of time on each concept, their understanding of it might be limited or they will likely forget the steps that they learned when going back to review old lessons.

Mixing the fast-paced lessons such as worksheets and flashcards with slower lessons provides a good balance. Whether your child is in kindergarten or is a senior in high school, there are all kinds of teaching techniques to take advantage of. The following methods for teaching mathematics offer a homemade feel for any child's individualized education and bring the subject of mathematics to life in a homey way.

Kitchen Math

It sounds cliché when homeschoolers mention that math can be easily learned in the kitchen and how not all math has to be done through worksheets. It might make parents sound like they are not taking homeschooling seriously enough, but that couldn't be further from the truth.

When one of my teenagers was doubling a recipe for cookies, she wanted to know how to easily double two-thirds of a cup of butter without just dumping in that amount two separate times. She had learned how to add fractions before in math, but as soon as it needed to be applied to real life, she was dumbfounded. That is why teaching the hands-on skills in the first place will both teach the concept and how to apply it in other areas of life. Aside from those benefits, children normally love being in the kitchen helping and learning with mom. Whether your child is young and discovering how to mix cookie dough, or your child is older and learning how to make the family's favorite dish, memories are being created in one of the best rooms of the house.

Kitchen Math Activities

Counting & Other Basic Math

- Count eggs, berries, hot dogs, etc.
- Practice subtraction by counting how many ingredients are left after using some.
- Teach addition by adding additional toppings to a pizza.
- Divide portions of a snack so that every person has an equal amount.
- Multiply to see how many cupcakes need to be made in order for everyone to have a certain amount.

Weight & Volume

- Use a kitchen scale to find out how much foods weigh.
- Learn how to convert volume to weight, such as how much one cup of rice weighs or vice versa.
- Calculate the cost of fruits and vegetables with a made-up price per weight amount.

Fractions

- Practice cutting food into specific fractions.
- Add, subtract, multiply, and divide fractions with measuring cups.
- See what a mixed number looks like by using two measuring cups (one full cup and a fraction in the other).

Conversions, Ratios, & Proportions

- Learn to convert measurements, such as how many tablespoons make one cup.
- Display a small poster with kitchen measurements and their conversions.
- Talk about a recipe and the ratio of its ingredients, such as two eggs per batch.
- Show how a ratio can be turned into a proportion to figure out how many more ingredients it will take to double or triple a recipe.

Grocery Budgeting

- Make a pretend grocery list with a realistic budget. Think about meals, snacks, and drinks. Draft up the list, then use a store app to go shopping and see the total cost at the end. If the budget is exceeded, fix the list by using substitute items or deleting items.
- Homemade vs. store-bought. Is it cheaper to make certain items yourself?
- Learn how coupons work.
- Talk about the importance of keeping receipts for a short period in case a food item is bad and needs to be returned. Also, teach how to contact manufacturers for free coupons if there was an issue with a product. Discuss how quality is sometimes worth more than quantity if one can afford it.

Math with Nature

Take your children out of their chairs and into the natural world to learn about things like patterns, geometry, fractions, data, graphing, and so much more. Nature gives children an environment where they can move around and learn with all of their senses. The best part about studying math outdoors is the simplicity of it. Using a mix of natural and practical items provides tools for so many different math concepts. Create a homeschool space in your own backyard or fill a basket to take with you and your children anywhere in nature. The beach, a forest, or a nearby park are all suitable areas.

Nature Math Supplies

- Clipboards
- Notebook
- Graph paper
- Index cards or cardstock
- Rocks with numbers drawn on them
- Wooden numbers
- Twine, rope, and yarn
- Chalk, paint, and pencils
- Paintbrushes
- Cardboard
- Ruler, yardstick, and measuring tape
- Measuring cups and spoons
- Small shovel
- Balance scale
- Timer and clock
- Rubber bands
- Popsicle sticks
- Outdoor thermometer
- Ice cube tray
- Pie tins and cake pans
- Sticks
- Acorns, chestnuts, walnuts, and seeds
- Leaves, bark, driftwood, and wood slices
- Gathering baskets, reusable bag, or paper bags
- White cloth 100 chart

Counting Activities

Make a Number Line

- Use cardstock squares, a marker, twine, and a hole puncher.
- Draw numbers on each square.
- Hang between two trees, on a fence, pegboard, or another area.
- Use it for counting, skip counting, adding, or subtraction.

Make a One Hundred Chart

- Use a square piece of white cloth.
- With a measuring stick and marker, draw a one hundred chart without the numbers.
- Use wooden or magnet numbers to fill it in and practice counting. It can easily be taken anywhere.

Number Rocks

- Collect smooth rocks.
- Draw numbers on each one, along with a plus, minus, and equal sign.
- Use as manipulatives to practice number recognition, counting, and basic math problems.

Multiplication & Division

Multiplication Visuals

- On a piece of paper, draw the number of circles that correlates with the math fact currently being worked on. Pick a number to multiply it by and fill each circle with that same number of nature items.

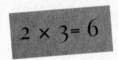

$2 \times 3 = 6$

Division Matching

- Using a cardboard square, write a list of division problems on one side with the answers mixed up on the other side.
- Use sticks to point to the correlating matches.

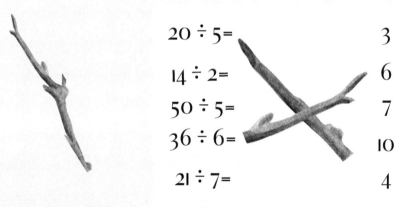

$20 \div 5 =$ 3

$14 \div 2 =$ 6

$50 \div 5 =$ 7

$36 \div 6 =$ 10

$21 \div 7 =$ 4

Chalk Word Problems

- Write a word problem on cement.
- Use real objects found in nature in the problem so that your child can use manipulatives to solve it, unless they are not needed.

Symmetry, Shapes, Patterns

Leaf Reflections

- Cut leaves vertically into halves.
- Attempt to draw the other side of the leaves, making them symmetrical.

Symmetry & Shape Hunt

- Explore different items in nature and look for the shapes that each contains.
- Check to see if they are symmetrical or not.

Make Shapes with Nature

- Collect items such as sticks, rocks, and leaves.
- Create different shapes using the collected items.

Make a Tessellation Pattern

- This kind of pattern happens when a surface is covered by a repeated shape, leaving no gaps. Turtles' shells do this.
- Make your own by drawing a honeycomb.

Pinecone Patterns

- Many pinecones have eight spirals going in one direction and thirteen going in the opposite direction. This is a type of pattern. Find pinecones near you and see if yours has the same pattern.

Graphing & Data

Plot Graph Growing Flowers

- Observe a flower growing every day for a set amount of time.
- Take the flower's height measurements each day.
- Record the flower's measurements on a plot graph. Note how the plot graph provides a quick visual to see if data is rising or falling.

Nature Bar Graphing

- Choose a type of item to record data on. For example, you can choose to compare different kinds of insects, trees, seeds, or flowers.
- Count how many of each item is in your yard or in a smaller contained area.
- Make and color a bar graph to record your findings.

Particpate in the Backyard Bird Count

- Every February 14-17, an organization called the Great Backyard Bird Count encourages people from all over the world to go outside for fifteen minutes per day and record the number of birds they notice, and label what kind they are. This helps scientists to better understand the birds around the world.

Fractions

Mud Kitchen Fractions:

- Provide blank wood slices and pretend to make pizza while dividing them into fractions with different toppings. Use leaves, grass, twigs, etc.
- Use measuring cups and spoons to pretend to make recipes.
- Use a cupcake pan to make pretend cupcakes with dirt and other natural items. Use a portion of the pan and discuss the fraction of cupcakes in it. Create different cupcake "flavors" with various natural items and name the number of cupcake flavors in fraction form.

Drawing Fractions:

- Cut wood slices into fractions for play.
- Paint one side of a wood slice with chalkboard paint, then practice drawing fractions with chalk.
- Use sticks to draw fractions in the soil or sand.

Magical Potions:

- Gather plastic bottles of different sizes. Use a marker to draw lines and label the outside with fraction measurements to visualize how much of the bottle is filled.
- Add ingredients of varying measuring cup sizes to the bottles such as water, glitter, pebbles, etc.

Real-life Math Projects

As children grow older, they need more playful options for learning that meet their maturity levels. Real-life math projects and activities let them use their imagination and creativity no matter what age they are.

Older children and teenagers might begin to ask more and more questions about why learning certain math concepts is really needed. There could also be some life skills related to math that you would like to teach as well. Realistic hands-on activities provide a solution to both of these situations. If you want to put a cozy twist on math for your growing children, come up with a project idea and spread out materials on the dining room table. Give them as much time as you can to dive deep into their projects, then let them present it to you when they are done. If they need help or want to do the activity together, use it as a teaching opportunity. Either way, completing math has the potential to be turned into a slow living kind of day.

There are so many math skills that can be brought to life, from area and perimeter to business math and carpentry. I've listed a few ideas to inspire you on the next page.

Real-life Math Activities

Roadside Stand Business:

- Build a temporary structure to place outside of your home or use a table and create a sign for your stand.
- Come up with a product list, such as baked goods, small plants that you have grown, homemade dog treats, jewelry, or jam.
- Figure out the cost of expenses and how much each unit should be priced at in order to make a profit.
- Create a monthly sales report document by listing how much revenue was received, the cost of expenses, and the net profit leftover.
- For an extension activity, research self-employment tax and figure out what percentage of the profit made would be owed to the government if it were a legitimate business.

Garden Box Blueprint & Model:

- Think of a design for a raised garden bed. You'll want to consider how many plants you'd like to plant and the space needed in between each one. The design can be rectangular or even L-shaped.
- Use graph paper to draw the blueprint, pretending that the squares are equivalent to square footage.
- Make a model out of cardboard, construction paper, popsicle sticks, and tissue paper.

Roadside Stand Inspiration

Chapter 8

Social Studies

Social studies covers a handful of subjects such as history, civics, economics, geography, anthropology, political science, and philosophy. It's funny how when I was a child in school, I could care less about these subjects unless an interesting fact stuck out to me. Now that I am older, I love learning more about these subjects and teaching them to my own kids. I have a goal to teach them better than I was taught in a way that strengthens connections to the topics at hand so that they actually come away with some meaningful knowledge about our country and the rest of the world.

There is so much to be learned that it is impossible to teach children everything related to social studies during their formal years of schooling. The amount taught, though, could be focused more on a child's understanding of events, places, and how life today has come to be, instead of merely memorizing facts of dates and every person's name that is read about. Homeschooling allows mothers to take their time teaching these subjects and make it beautiful in the process.

Social Studies Through Books

My favorite way to teach social studies is through books. When I started out with homeschooling, I visited a bookstore to look for teaching materials such as curriculum choices. I strolled back to the large children's section and never expected to find that almost every topic that would be in a typical social studies curriculum was available in many forms. I peeked through the storybooks and found that there were various books available in chronological order in history. Beautiful illustrations filled the pages and the information inside explained events in a way that was not only easy for children to understand, but was also engaging.

As I approached the next section of shelves, I found that chapter books existed as well. Historical fiction that allowed the reader to peer into a first-person point of view of a character who was experiencing a significant time in history, political event, or cultural shift was available by the dozens. Non-fiction chapter books made typical textbooks look much more boring than they already had appeared.

What I noticed when skimming through all of these books were the details given. Zoning in on a single topic allowed for much more knowledge to be unleashed compared to other teaching materials. It made me wonder what could be done with those resources. Could a textbook or a list of "need-to-know" concepts be the spine for what I teach, while pulling the actual information from regular books? I weighed the pros and cons. On one hand, I would be teaching my children in a non-conventional way and doing so would not allow us to get through each topic as quickly. The pros were the exact same reasons as the cons. After all, I had never desired to move as fast as possible through my children's education.

My kids are currently on summer break, and like every other homeschool mom at this time, I'm working on gathering ideas and planning for the upcoming school year. My oldest, who will be a senior, does not need a social studies credit for twelfth grade as it is not required, but it is optional. Since she loves reading about historical events that interest her, I've come up with an idea. It is already a tradition for my oldest and me to have our own time studying together at a local bookstore and cafe once per week. For a history credit, she is to choose a history-themed book from within the bookstore and read through some of it to learn about that specific topic. We usually spend a few hours at the bookstore, so she can read a decent amount if she sticks to the same topic for a couple of weeks. Aside from reading books, other resources can be added in at home, such watching videos, reading online articles, writing about what she will have learned, and one or two assignments I come up with.

Young children can enjoy picture books related to social studies that are read like a story, while older children can do the same but in a way that is at their level. Non-fiction books are available for any age and are more likely to catch a child's interest compared to studying a basic textbook. Topics such as the Titanic, Area 51, or women inventors can easily be found. I often stroll the library for books related to the topics we are studying and I'm usually not disappointed with what I find.

The amount of homeschooling companies has vastly grown over the years. As a result, many have created exactly what homeschoolers want...a social studies curriculum that is based around literature. If you want a more organized way to teach through books, picking a curriculum like that may be helpful.

Drawing Through Social Studies

Artists, doodlers, or even children who are willing to try something creative may find drawing activities enlightening as opposed to a classic assignment. To start, provide a dedicated sketchbook to your child. After a lesson is taught, direct them to draw something related to what they learned.

If presidential elections are the topic, then political cartoons could be a good idea to create. If the Mayflower is the focus of a history discussion, they could attempt to draw the boat. Written words are not necessary for this activity, but are optional to add to the drawing. If you prefer that your child also writes a corresponding paragraph or something similar, they could draw on one page of their sketchbook and use the next page for writing. The point of this activity is to retain information that is learned as it may be easier for some children to remember something when it is drawn. Drawing through social studies is also a slow enough activity to take their time on.

Hands-On History

Tinkerers and makers love being able to build their assignments as opposed to alternative methods. Children who usually don't desire to complete these kinds of activities might be surprised to find out the fun they can have with them. While teaching at a homeschool co-op a few years ago, I had the children make artificial poppy flowers using felt as they learned about the First World War in the United States. They also constructed models of bomb shelters using cardstock, popsicle sticks, and mini toy soldiers.

Hands-on activities can also include art. In the past, my children have made replicas of stone tablets from the Mesopotamian times by using clay and then carving scribes onto them with toothpicks. Another idea I've seen recently is cloth dyeing like the American pioneers once did. They used fruits and vegetables to make dyes in order to put color into clothing and other items.

Almost any lesson in history can take advantage of a hands-on approach, whether it's an engineering activity, art project, or model making. It has the potential to be a child's favorite part about studying history.

Exploring Geography Through Cooking

A lot can be learned from exploring the different foods of many cultures and geographic locations. Although we cannot travel to all the places our world has to offer, we can get a glimpse into the lives of other people by exploring their typical food dishes and the culture that surrounds them.

Whether you want to plan a "foods around the world" day or explore one place at a time, all it takes is a little preparation. Once you choose an area to focus on, pick one or two recipes. You'll want to try to choose foods that your children can help make for the most immersive experience. To learn more about the specific place, find and print an information worksheet with some questions attached to it or print a fun activity sheet. Then, choose a book to read aloud or a video to watch before getting started with making the food. Including a craft that corresponds with the chosen topic can be a fun but optional addition. Some other ideas for you and your children to research when studying your chosen topic are finding out what foods are a staple in a typical family's household, their favorite snacks, the usual times they eat meals, and holiday food options.

Foods From Different Places

Countries of the World

- Poland- pierogis
- Netherlands- speculaas
- Spain- jalapeño cornbread
- Ireland- shepherd's pie

- China- cream cheese fried wontons
- Thailand- chicken lettuce wraps
- Germany- potato soup

- India- garlic naan bread
- Italy- Italian wedding soup
- Japan- clear soup
- Mexico- Mexican street corn

- Canadia- pancakes
- France- soufflé dessert

American Dishes

- Chicago style hotdog
- New York style pizza
- Southern biscuits and gravy, fried chicken and waffles, baked macaroni and cheese, collard greens, fried green tomatoes, and chicken pot pie
- Michigan coney dog with chili sauce
- California cobb salad, animal fries, grilled pork chop with cherry sauce, and cioppino
- Florida key lime pie, coconut patties, Cuban sandwich, and freshly-squeezed orange juice

Planning a Unit Study for Time Periods

A unit study is an organized plan for teaching a specific topic. If you are wanting to deepen your children's knowledge of a certain time period in history, this can be a fun and interesting way of accomplishing that goal. I also love how a full unit study can be a slow and intentional way of teaching.

To plan your very own unit study, you'll want to make some lists. A library list for books on the chosen time period, related movies or documentaries to watch, videos and online articles that offer more information, projects, activities, recipes, assignments, famous documents or speeches, and report ideas are good lists to make. Once that is done, you'll want to realistically narrow down your lists for what you actually want to complete and make a schedule for when it will all happen.

An add-in that may be helpful for your children to retain some of the new information they learn is a dedicated notebook. They can use it to make a timeline of events as they go through the unit study. Other things to include in the notebook are a vocabulary list, drawings of maps, answers to questions that you provide them with, and written essays.

If you want to get creative with your unit study, add in a skit that your child can write and perform, recreate a piece of art from history, or sketch a design for a piece of clothing from another decade. When studying the 1960s, my daughter took a pair of old jeans, cut a slit on the sides at the bottom, then sewed in a piece of fabric with a colorful pattern so that they looked like hippy bell bottoms. Another idea is to assign a creative writing assignment that involves having to write a short historical fiction piece based on a specific time period. This could give your child the opportunity to imagine what it was like to be a young person during the period they are studying.

Having a party with your children is another creative route you can take. Make costumes, play games that other children played during the chosen time in history, and have a lunch or dinner with foods from that time as well. If you want to go big, plan a friends and family party where you invite other people to your party. Think of what fun an English tea party or a Medieval dinner party would be.

When looking at history's time periods, so many teaching opportunities can be taken advantage of. Instead of viewing them as another chapter in a textbook to get through, visualize them as a unique learning experience to ponder for a while. I've put together a list of time periods below for you to refer back to when planning future history lessons. I've also included a sample of a unit study on pages 139-141 for the Colonial period.

Major Time Periods in History

- The Stone Age
- The Bronze Age
- The Iron Age
- The Classical Era
- The Medieval Era
- The Early Modern Era
- The Modern Era

A Unit Study for the Colonial Period

Study the European colonization of America, better known as the "colonial times," that took place between 1607 and 1783 in North America creating a unit study that is centered around that time period.

Book List

- *If You Lived in Colonial Times* by Ann McGovern
- *Who Was Betsy Ross?* by James Buckley Jr.
- *The Witch of Blackbird Pond* by Elisabeth George Speare
- *Scar* by J. Albert Mann
- *George Washington's Spy* by Elvira Wolf

What to Watch

- *Liberty Kids* TV Series
- BrainPOP: Building the Thirteen Colonies

Vocabulary Words to Study

- Quaker
- Frontier
- Jamestown
- Roanoke
- Colonize
- Settler
- Settlement
- Britain

Cook Cast Iron Johnny Cakes

- Cast iron skillet
- Cooking spray
- 1 cup of cornmeal
- 1/2 tsp of salt
- 1 cup of boiling water
- 1/2 cup of milk
- Butter and honey for toppings

Directions

1. Mix the cornmeal and salt together in a medium bowl.
2. Stir in boiling water.
3. Add the milk, then stir well.
4. Drop spoonfuls into the skillet.
5. Cook for 4 minutes, then flip and cook for another 4 minutes.
6. Serve with butter and honey on top.

Make a Betsy Ross Flag

- Place 7 red strips of paper onto a white piece of paper, making 13 stripes total.
- Place a blue paper rectangle in one corner.
- With a white crayon, draw 13 stars in a circular shape on the blue rectangle.

Make Hole-Punched Tin Lanterns

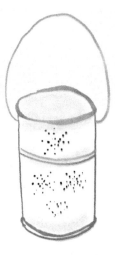

Step 1:

To create a hard surface to hammer, fill the can with water and place it in the freezer overnight.

Step 2:

With your marker, draw a design by marking the outside of the can with dots to form a pattern.

Step 3:

After placing your can on a folded towel, proceed to use a nail and hammer to punch holes into the design.

Step 4:

Punch two holes into each side of the can towards the top for the handles. Use the wire to thread through the holes, bending at the ends so they stay in place.

Step 5:

Let the can soak in hot water so the ice melts and loosens easily from the can.

Step 6: Place your tea light inside.

Supplies:

- Tin can with one end removed
- Permanent marker
- Towel
- Hammer
- Large nail
- Bendable metal wire (1 foot long)
- Tea light candle (real or battery operated to play with)

Chapter 9

Science

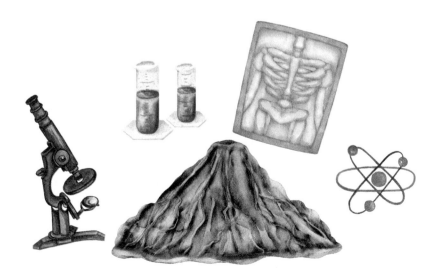

Sibling Science

Although children of different ages are obviously at different levels when it comes to studying science, topics in this subject can be easily given to multiple age levels at the same time, making homeschooling much simpler. The same concept can be taught while also altering the lesson plan so that older children gain more out of it.

Young children grasp on to more than we sometimes think they do. A book that can be read aloud to a fourth grader can still be read aloud to a first grader. There may be some words that the first grader does not understand, but they can either be explained during or after the book has been read. Even if they do not understand every single aspect of the book, the parts that they are ready to will stick along with some new vocabulary words or knowledge that they did not know before. Aside from reading books together, books for different readers can be easily gathered on the same topic through your local library. While teaching my children about fungi, my high schooler read a scientific chapter book written by a researcher about the hidden world of mushrooms, while my youngest child looked at picture books which illustrated the parts of a mushroom. My oldest used her tablet to draw a digital diagram of a mushroom, and my youngest colored a printable of one while matching the names of each part to its corresponding location.

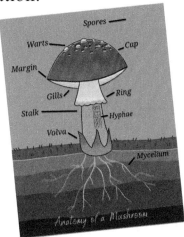

When planning an activity for my children to do together, I gave them a mushroom scavenger hunt to complete while taking a nature walk. We also learned about safe and unsafe fungi, how to forage it properly, and the types that exist in the location that we live in. Combining lessons simplifies science and gives children the opportunity to explore new topics together.

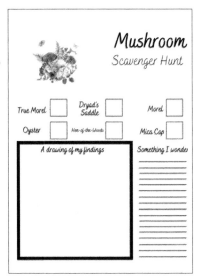

145

Slow Living Science Books

A slow living science book is one that a child can bask in for a while. It either engages, piques curiosity, or entertains. If such books exist, then why shouldn't they be the main text-based source of scientific information?

Usually, a slow living science book will either focus on one specific topic, such as the night stars. They can also focus on a much broader topic, like all about the Earth or a full book about chemistry. One example of a slow living science book is some children's reference books. These should be full books packed with photos, facts, and interesting information. Sometimes, they might even contain activity ideas and instructions. Another example is a family style science book. This kind offers text that can be read aloud to the whole family and contains activities that can be done together. Lastly, scientific narratives are another type of this kind of book. Complete fiction that is based on facts, actual true stories told like a story, or first-person experiences are all excellent sources of information that allow children to learn important concepts in a slower way.

Homeschool Mom Collaboration

It's hard to take on science completely on your own. The supplies can become pricey, experiments take a lot of preparation and time, and some homeschool moms might not love the idea of dissecting a frog. Throughout my homeschooling years, I have found ways to make science simpler without sacrificing my children's education.

A few years ago when my daughter started high school, biology was the first scientific subject to tackle. The experiments for that grade level definitely stepped up their game and I was nervous about it. When a fellow homeschool mom reached out to me about getting our teenagers together to complete some science experiments, a weight was lifted off my shoulders. This particular mom enjoyed completing hands-on activities and made bigger projects such as dissecting a frog, less intimidating. If you meet another homeschool mom who has a child in the same grade as yours, it might be a wise idea to collaborate on certain science activities together. It could also benefit your child to have a lab partner as well.

Community Resources

Sometimes you have to think outside of the box when it comes to teaching science to your homeschoolers. Putting together a list of resources from outside of your home can provide a well-rounded science curriculum.

I don't live in a big city that has a science museum, a planetarium, or endless science activities. But even while living in a small town, I have been able to gather some really good things that have served as a supplement for science. Our nature center offers affordable summer activities for children of all ages that involve hiking, exploring, tree identification, learning about poisonous plants, etc. Our library hosts free STEM nights, hands-on science projects, and special speakers that discuss specific topics. A local wilderness group invites children every week from the spring to autumn to come and play around the ponds and identify insects and plant life. A gardening center has hosted bee discussions where attendees were able to make their own bee house while learning about pollination. Finding activities in your area not only gives your children more fun ways to learn about science but also allows experts in their fields to share knowledge with them in real-life.

Host a Homeschool Science Fair

Some activities that are usually held in schools can be easily adapted for the homeschool community. What I like most about doing this is the ability to change the traditional way of doing such activities just because, as homeschool moms, we can. Besides experiments being the main requirement of a science fair, why not allow some more creativity as well?

During the time that I was the leader for a homeschool teen group, I hosted a science fair that allowed homeschoolers from all over our area to participate for free. I used a free space at our community library and shared information about it on social media. The purpose was to let homeschoolers show off their knowledge and skills while giving their families an opportunity to support them at a special event. The participants were able to make displays about anything science-related, whether it be a model, diagram, presentation, experiment, or even an artistic replica. The science fair was filled with proud relatives who were entertained while walking through the fair, observing every homeschooler's hard work.

Chapter 10

Enrichment Studies

Strewing

After years of homeschooling, I finally had some space in my home to set up a homeschool area. I had always dreamt of what it would look like. A big table for all of my kids and me to sit together, shelving that displays current learning themes, educational toys, a vintage poster with the Pledge of Allegiance, beautiful books, and a nature shelf are some of the things I yearned for. When I transformed a large room into a mix of a dining area, homeschool space, and my writing spot, my vision came to life.

Soon I'd be frequently picking things up from yard sales, thrift stores, and snagging Amazon deals. Things like puzzles, kits, or any toy that could be incorporated into a learning theme of some kind were so easy and cheap to obtain. Oftentimes, I could find things around the house too. Since my homeschoolers' lessons would change frequently, I was always wanting to put out different items for them to learn with or to discover. I then realized that the same idea could be applied to their interests or even potential interests as well. I set out my son's musical play instruments along with printed lyrics to his favorite songs, and I dug out an old keyboard from a closet. Another time, I filled a basket with pretend frogs and flies, small pieces of driftwood, and a piece of blue felt to mimic a pond. Little by little, these items didn't only stay in our homeschool space. There would be a book basket in the living room with books I would change out frequently and different storytelling items such as finger puppets, printed and laminated paper dolls, or props to match a story. A crochet tray was located in another room and a box of tinker toys was in the garage. We had a basket that was always packed and ready to go outside, including a shovel to dig with, bug-catching supplies, and a sketchbook and nature guide for my oldest.

Even though gathering simple items and scattering them throughout your home for your children to find may seem unimpactful, it's absolutely not. For some reason, when this method is used, children see things through a new set of lenses. Something that was useless before is now inspiring their imagination. Maybe a certain topic that your children wouldn't have caught their attention before has now piqued their interest.

For a long time I had no idea that what I was partaking

it was something called strewing, which means to scatter about. In the homeschool world, it means to scatter different items around your home or homeschool area for your children to find and put to use. The purpose is to serve as an enrichment to their learning.

Passion Baskets

Homeschooling gives children the ability to have more time left in the day. Core subjects often do not take as long when done at home versus a traditional classroom, leaving a much larger window of time that can be used for other activities. On days when there is nothing else going on after completing lessons, such as sports, cooperatives, or playdates, I came up with the idea of a passion basket. Each child receives their own and we fill it together. We choose something they want to learn about or a topic/skill that they are passionate about and want to build upon. More than one type of interest can be combined as well. Then, we will fill it with correlating items.

For example, if your child is interested in crocheting, add a how-to book or a book of crochet project ideas, hooks, yarn, and measuring

154

tape. If he or she wants to learn about wilderness skills, fill it with a related activity book, any needed supplies, plant and tree identification for the area you live in, and animal tracking memorization cards.

Passion baskets can serve a few different purposes. They give children an incentive to finish their regular school work and are a task to look forward to. They fill in gaps of time with a meaningful activity that is still leisurely, as opposed to turning to electronics. Old-fashioned elective subjects could potentially be replaced with a passion basket if you feel it is deemed appropriate. Lastly, passion baskets teach children how to make time to invest in themselves and what they like to do or become knowledgeable of.

Service to Others

What if everyone actively sought out ways to serve others? There is no doubt that the world would be brighter. We may not be able to encourage every person to do that, but we could make a world of difference if we start in our own home. Children can be taught to see the power in helping others if we take on the task alongside them. Use the list on the next page to be inspired.

Serve Others With Your Children

Friends and Family

- Prepare and deliver a meal when someone is going through a hard time.
- Check up on people who don't receive much company.
- Offer to do a chore that they don't have time for.

Neighbors

- Make a decorative wreath as a gift.
- Babysit for a family in need.
- Organize craft activities in a park for the neighborhood children.
- Bring a neighbor's trash cans back up to their house on windy days when they aren't home.
- Invite a child to play if they don't have many friends.

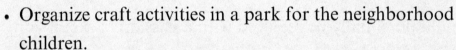

Community

- Throw monthly birthday parties for nursing home residents.
- Drop off baked goods to the librarians.
- Make dog treats for an animal shelter.
- Build a little library in front of your home.
- Drop off coloring books and crayons to hospital emergency rooms.
- Have a garage sale and use the money to organize and host a special activity for homeschoolers in your area.

Homeschool Events

Special events aren't just for children who attend school. In fact, when homeschool parents work together, they have the ability to experiment with all different kinds of them. In the past, my homeschool community has held a spelling bee, an art fair, a color run, monthly book clubs, a bonfire teen night, etc. Usually, other parents are excited to hear when a fellow homeschool mom is taking the initiative to get something started, and some may even be willing to help as well.

 Event Ideas

- Puzzle competition
- Cardboard engineering
- Handmade market
- Outside movie on a projector
- Craft club
- Escape room
- Fishing trip
- Field day
- Nature walk
- Spring formal dance

- Spelling bee
- Talent show
- Flag football game
- Arcade night
- Bowling
- Put on a small play
- Poetry reading
- Color run
- Bonfire with s'mores
- Super Bowl watch party
- Family picnic

Electives

Electives aren't considered to be core subjects, but are more like classes that enrich a child's education. While many states require or suggest certain types of electives, parents can usually customize them as much as they wish.

Homeschooling also allows the opportunity to explore unique topics and skills that would otherwise be offered by a school. For example, physical education does not have to look like a typical gym class routine. Taking walks, bike riding, roller skating, using a gym membership, playing basketball with friends, or classes at your local recreation department can all be used as a physical education credit.

Foreign languages can branch out further into any area of interest. Latin, Swedish, or even American Sign Language can replace the typical subjects that other children tend to learn when in middle or high school. If a specific topic or event from history is appealing to a child, it can be easily turned into an elective, especially ones that are not mentioned at all in homeschool textbooks.

Don't ever think that electives are not important. They are sometimes the heart of a child's education.

Elective Ideas

- Women's history
- Mythology
- Natural history
- Inventors
- How things are made
- Engineering
- Carpentry
- Coding
- Robotics
- Programming
- Digital art
- Graphic design
- Animation
- Art history
- Pottery
- Architecture
- Woodworking
- Blacksmithing
- Auto mechanics
- Sociology
- Foreign languages
- Filmmaking
- Typing
- Animal care
- Photography
- Music theory
- Instrument lessons
- Voice lessons
- Fashion design
- Interior design
- Bowling lessons
- Video game design
- Cake baking & decorating
- Sewing & alterations
- Crochet & knitting
- Self-defense
- Martial arts
- Sports
- Weight lifting
- Archery
- Target shooting
- Hunting
- Consumer Math
- Financial literacy
- Life skills
- Religion study
- Take a co-op class
- College dual enrollment
- Create your own course

Chapter 11

Nature & Wonder Through the Seasons

How to Use this Guide

With each changing season, there is so much to delight in.
Nature shifts through different phases right before our eyes.
Mothers can harness these miracles through a simplified
nature study. It does not have to be overly technical and
should be enjoyed by every child, no matter how young or
old. There is such a vast amount of knowledge that it is
impossible to learn everything at once, if ever at all. Don't
think of each topic in nature as a task of information to
check off. Instead, demonstrate to your children how to
soak in the little details of the seasons, observe nature, and
learn something new.

The following guide contains six weeks of various nature
topics for each season, along with some special activities. I
suggest looking ahead each week to see if any supplies are
needed. You'll also need to either use the internet or a
nature field guide to read a little bit about each topic or
watch a video on it. Lastly, each child needs a nature
journal with blank paper to draw and write on. Some basic
craft supplies such as chalk pastels, watercolor paints, and
colored pencils are required.

Homeschooling in the Fall

Homeschooling in the Fall is a special time of year.

It reminds mothers of how everything they cherish is near.

Instead of the times when sending children away is the norm,

They choose to keep them close, through the Autumn storms.

As the children come rumbling down the old creaky stairs,

The thought of rushing to the bus is without any cares.

Each day, the goal is to start simply and slowly.

It's a blessing to be able to, the mothers comprehend fully.

The cold, hard desks are replaced with soft comfy chairs,

The cafeteria, substituted with mom's cooking in the air.

All the nooks and crannies are where books can be found,

And are meant to be read when the children gather around.

The Fall season comes once per year,

And reminds mothers why they hold homeschooling so dear.

Week 1: Trees

- Go on a nature walk in an area where various trees are around. Collect leaves from three different trees. Notice the ground surrounding each chosen tree. Are there any seeds or pinecones that have fallen? If so, collect a sample of those too.
- Use a tree identification field guide to figure out what kind of trees you collected from. Use the internet to find out why leaves change colors.
- In your nature journal, draw and label each leaf and/or seeds and other findings. A leaf rubbing with crayons is also optional.
- While on a walk, have a gratitude scavenger hunt. Find and name things in nature that you are thankful for, make you happy, or enjoy to look at.

Week 2: Spiders

- Find a spider web outside. They can usually be found in small spaces, in between branches, or on a porch railing. Notice how perfectly designed it is.
- Try to draw the spider web in your nature journal.
- Learn about the life cycle of a spider online. Draw and label a diagram of the life cycle in your journal.
- Talk about what life lessons can be learned from a spider. For example: there is beauty in the handmade.

Week 3: Harvest Moon

- The full moon that occurs closest to the Autumnal Equinox is called the Harvest Moon. It appears brighter than other full moons because of the way the Earth is tilting. In the Northern Hemisphere, the Harvest Moon can be viewed in September, but sometimes in October.
- Gather storybooks and educational books from the library about the Harvest Moon and look at them throughout the week.
- Go on a nighttime nature walk when the Moon is visible.
- Using chalk pastels, make an illustration of the moon on a dark blue piece of construction paper. Draw orange, yellow, and red leaves floating around the moon so that they look like they are blowing in the wind.
- Search online about how the Harvest Moon got it's name.

Week 4: Autumn Equinox

- Find out the times that the sun sets and rises on this day in your location. What's happening in other locations?
- Looking out your window or while outside, paint your own illustration of Autumn.
- Make a centerpiece by filling a vase with pinecones, acorns, and add cinnamon sticks or essential oils to create a nice scent.
- Have a Fall bonfire or make a pot of chili together to celebrate the season.

Week 5: Seeds

- During this time of year, bulbs can be planted to prepare for Spring.
- Talk about how seeds are moved around in their environment and get from place to place. (Animals, wind, erosion)
- Using pumpkin, maple, and sunflower seeds, create a mosaic design with glue and a small canvas or cardstock. Ideas for what image to make could include a leaf, pumpkin, or other Fall-inspired objects.

Week 6: Mushrooms

- Check out a book from the library that lists different types of mushrooms and how to forage them or use the internet. to learn how.
- Go on a nature walk and try to find different types of mushrooms and identify them.
- In your nature journal, draw a mushroom you have found, write down where you found it, and what kind it could be.
- Set up a nature altar on a shelf, table, or desk by collecting different items on a walk. Another idea is to fill a glass bottle or vase with these items and use it as a decoration. Tie an orange or green ribbon around the bottle for an extra touch.

Feast in Nature's Company

Autumn presents us with the grand feast of the year, offering a variety of produce and flavors ready for the taking. It's a season when gardens and orchards brim with plenty, making it the perfect time to come together with your children for a charming picnic amidst the falling leaves and cool breeze.

Choose a cozy spot, whether it's under the comforting shade of a grand tree or next to a sparkling lake. Spread out a blanket and let nature's artwork set the scene for your meal. Infuse your picnic with the essence of autumn by including freshly picked apples with a side of caramel, warm or cold apple cider, and maybe a thermos of wild rice and vegetable soup in your basket.

Add in a touch of nature studies by encouraging your children to utilize their nature journals to draw and write about what they see around them. Perhaps write a poem for a writing activity as well. Let the autumn season surround you while sharing stories and laughter together.

Winter

Homeschooling in the Winter

Homeschooling in the winter brings all kinds of cozy things.

Stacks of books in all the nooks.

Snowy sights and warm candlelights.

The scent of comfort dishes as the kettle hisses.

Snowy play outside and cuddling together inside.

We hibernate within our home as it snows

while listening to the sound of the north wind as it blows.

Week 1: Preparing for Winter

- Go on a nature walk and look at the trees around you. Notice how the branches look. Do they have buds on them?
- Collect pieces of nature for your nature table/shelf. Replace your Fall items with the Winter items.
- Illustrate a Winter scene using only white chalk pastels.
- Find old coats, scarves, and gloves in your home that can be donated to a homeless shelter.

Week 2: Winter Solstice

- Look for signs of Winter on a nature walk. Things to look for are bright red berries, animal tracks in the snow or soft soil, and visible birds' nests in the bare trees.
- Record the times that the sun sets and rises in your location.
- Make paper snowflakes with paper, scissors, and glitter. Hang them with clear fishing line from your ceiling.

Week 3: Pinecones

- Go on a nature walk in an area where pine trees are located and collect some pinecones. Try to find different kinds.
- Using the internet, research the different types of pinecones and what trees they come from.
- In your nature journal, recreate the drawing below of the life cycle of a pine tree.

Sapling

Young Tree

Pinecone

Adult Tree

Week 4: Animal Tracking

- Choose a nearby nature trail to walk where there is also either snow or soft soil on the ground.
- Have a camera available on your walk and take photos of any tracks you notice on the ground. Use an animal tracking guide or the internet to identify the tracks you have found.
- Draw the tracks or print and tape your photos inside of your journal.
- For fun, sketch a made-up print from a mysterious unknown animal.

How to Track Animals

Explain to your children that people from long ago used to have to depend on their animal tracking skills in order to hunt and gather food. Today, hunters still use these exact same skills, and children can try it too, for fun! Make a game out of it by telling your children that tracking animals is similar to solving a mystery. What animal has been here? What were they doing? Where did it go and where did it come from?

Animal tracks are easiest to find in mud, soft soil, sand, and snow. A great place to look for tracks is near a bird feeder because birds sometimes hop in the snow or mud under the feeder. Squirrels and mice are known for visiting these areas too as they try to eat the seeds that have fallen from the feeder.

When your child finds an animal track, tell them to observe the shape of it and whether or not it also has toe marks. Have them draw it in a journal. There are tons of field guides you can purchase or borrow from the library to help you identify the tracks. Look for one that specifically is for the area you live in, such as "Northeast United States."

Week 5: Owls

- Purchase an owl pellet kit to dissect.
- For elementary children, read the cute book *Ruthie and Ozzy Owl* by Sandra Dersa.
- For middle grades and high schoolers, read *What an Owl Knows* by Jennifer Ackerman.
- To make an owl nature craft, you will need a 5x7 piece of cardboard, tacky glue or hot glue, and items from nature such as small twigs, acorns, seeds, and light pebbles. Draw an outline of an owl on the cardboard. Copy the illustration of the owl below if needed. Fill the owl in by gluing your nature items onto it.

Week 6: Hibernation

- Look up the following vocabulary words and discuss their definitions or copy them into your nature journal:

1. Hibernation
2. Torpor
3. Brumation
4. Diapause
5. Hibernaculum

- Make a graph comparing the statistics of bats and bears and how they hibernate. Answer the questions such as, how long each hibernates for, if either of them wakes up in between, weight gain, and heart rates.

- Write a poem about the photo below or recreate the photograph using any kind of medium, such as paint or colored pencils.

Staying Warm in the 1700s

Discuss how people used to stay warm before modern inventions came about by reading the passage below. Answer the questions aloud together.

A Colonial Winter

During the Colonial times in America, many might imagine families huddled around a cozy fire for warmth. While it may seem like a simpler time, it probably took a lot more effort than we realize. Fireplaces were the primary heat source back then, leading to a daily struggle to stay warm. Constant wood collection was necessary, yet even with fires burning all day, houses could remain very cold. Without servants and slaves, bedrooms and larger areas like the dining room often went without heat. Typically, the smallest space or the common living room was kept heated. At night, blankets were piled on to stay warm, along with wearing wool or thick clothing (Rogers, J. 2021). Day-to-day life must have been taxing during the Winter months.

Comprehension Questions

1. What was one type of clothing people would wear to stay warm?
2. Why was it hard to keep homes warm back then?
3. Why do you think people who had slaves probably had a warmer house?
4. Pretend like you are a child living during that time period. Write a short diary entry describing one of your days.

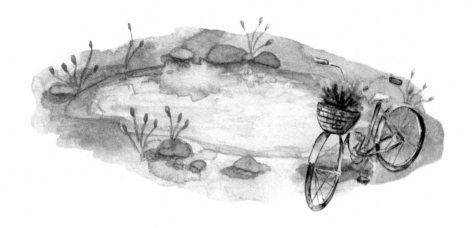

Homeschooling in the Spring

The time has come

to hear the birds hum.

We open the windows while working on our lesson.

Slow living is our only intention.

When the flowers sprout,

we hurry and go out.

Nature studies are waiting.

In the Spring sun, we'll be bathing.

Week 1: Birds

- During this time of year, the birds are very active. You'll see many of them working to build nests for their up-and-coming baby birds. Go in your backyard and take some time to observe a bird. Do you see it grabbing grass and other natural materials to take back to a tree? They might also be using a hole in a tree trunk or a crevice in a house to make their nests. Birds will spend all day collecting items until their nest is just right.

- In your journal, write down the kinds of birds you saw. Use your field guide or the internet if you need to identify them. Write about what you saw them doing and list what natural materials they collected if you see any.

- To help the birds in your yard, put out things such as moss, yarn, or clippings near a bird feeder. They will be likely to use them.

Week 2: Flowers

- Look for the first blooms of the season while on a walk or in your own yard. Tulips are one of the first flowers to bloom during this time.

- Choose a flower that you find and try to identify it with your field guide or the internet.

- Make a poster with a drawing of the flower you chose and write some facts about it after researching online or in a book. Label the parts of the flower as well.

Week 3: Pond Study

- In the Spring, pond life is emerging. Tadpoles, snails, and ducklings are being born. Find a shallow pond nearby and see what you can find.
- Pull up an illustration of a frog's life cycle online or in a book and copy it into your journal.
- Look up the difference between a toad and a frog and draw a Venn diagram in your journal to compare them.
- Read *The Adventures of Frog and Toad* to your younger children.
- Write a creative writing piece about a pond animal in a folk tale style. Folk tales have animals in their stories with human-like characteristics, such as being able to talk. If your child can't write yet, they can draw their story and you can add the words. If they can write, have them complete one to two pages.

Week 4: Clouds

- Clouds can determine different things. Will it rain, snow, or just cast a shadow on the Earth? But have you noticed that the shapes of clouds can greatly vary? This week, have a picnic on a dry day. Lay out and look at the sky.
- Draw in your nature journal what you see along with writing down details.
- Research the different types of clouds and try to identify the ones you saw on your picnic.

Week 5: The Colors of Spring

- Go on a walk and notice how everything around you is becoming more colorful than it was in the winter.
- Collect spring nature finds for your nature table/shelf.
- Write a poem about spring and its colors.
- Notice how the days are becoming longer. Record in your journal the time the sun sets and rises in your location.
- Learn why rainbows appear by looking in a book or on the internet.
- Using watercolors, paint a rainbow on a piece of paper.

Week 6: Caterpillars & Butterflies

- Visit an area known to have a lot of butterflies.
- Observe a butterfly's behavior and write about it in your journal. Identify it if you can as well.
- Read about the stages of growth of a caterpillar and how it turns into a butterfly. Sometimes if you walk through the forest in the Spring, you'll find caterpillars hanging in their cocoons from branches.
- Write your own inspirational quote about life that is inspired by butterflies. Help your child come up with one together if they can't think of one on their own.
- Create your own butterfly drawing using colored pencils. Try to make both sides symmetrical.

Prepare the Home for Spring

With Spring comes the freshness from the outdoors. Talk to your children about how it's a nice time to freshen up the inside of your home as well. From cleaning and organizing to adding a touch of Spring colors and scents, there is a lot that can be done to embrace the season and live through it intentionally.

Have your children pick out old toys they no longer want and then show them the importance of deep cleaning their rooms. Even the littlest children can participate by wiping down the baseboards. Older children can clean the windows and everyone can help strip the beds and get them into the wash at the same time.

Encourage your children to make Spring-themed art to hang on their walls. Pick a couple of flowers and display them in a vase on their dressers. Add a Spring aroma with a flower-scented air freshener. Your children will gain the experience of harmonizing their lives with the Spring season.

Summer

Homeschooling in the Summer

For some children, an education takes a slumber.

But for others, it can be the most profound during the summer.

It may not be all pencils and essays,

but it is full of lightning bugs and long beach days.

It is the time of the season

when learning takes place without any reason.

Don't view summer as a three-month break.

Look at it as just another piece of the homeschooling cake.

Week 1: Summer Solstice

- The Summer Solstice marks the longest day of the year. Go on a nature walk and look for signs of summer. You'll likely see wildflowers, more varieties of plants growing, and insects coming out to enjoy the warm temperatures.
- Take back some natural materials to set on your nature shelf/table.
- Record in your journal the time the sun sets and rises.
- Pick a nature item of your choice to sketch.

Week 2: Moths

- The variety of moths is vast. They are considered an insect that is a part of the order Lepidoptera. Even though they look similar, they are not butterflies. Female moths produce a distinct scent that male moths can smell from miles away. Moths are nocturnal, meaning they are active at night. They play an important role in our environment because they are one of the few pollinators that work during the night when others are sleeping.
- Moths are attracted to light and ripe fruit. Take a flashlight on a night walk and hold still for a little while. Eventually, you will most likely encounter a moth. Take a good look without touching it because their wings can be easily damaged.
- Research types of moths and make a mini poster with drawings of 6 kinds and label them.

Week 3: Night Sky

- Watch a video about constellations then research which one is easy to find in your location. Draw a picture of one in your nature journal.
- Plan a beach night and take a telescope with you if you have one. Try to find the constellation that you researched. Was it what you expected to see in real life? Write down your observations in your journal.
- Paint a night sky picture using black, blue, and white paint.

Week 4: Honeybees

- Some honeybees sting if they feel threatened, but they die immediately afterwards. Look up the following vocabulary words and write the definitions in your journal:
1. Queen bee
2. Male drone
3. Female worker bee
- The drones are the bees that collect nectar and fill a special stomach that they have with it. They fly back to their homes and empty the contents into a honeycomb. It then turns into honey as it thickens.
- If your child is younger, have them draw a poster with information about why we need to protect honeybees in our environment. If your child is older, have them write a three to five paragraph essay about why honeybees are important.

Week 5: Wildflowers

- Wildflowers are able to grow in the most rugged of places as they are extremely resilient and can flourish without the help of humans.
- Go on a walk where there could be wildflowers and try to identify one with your field guide or the internet.
- Write about the flower you chose in your journal and draw a picture of it. Write down details about its surroundings also.
- Collect some wildflowers to press and dry in a book or with a flower press.

Week 6: Summer Field Trip

- Choose a location that can immerse you in nature and enjoy the season. Perhaps somewhere you can hike, sightsee, swim, etc. Act like a nature photographer and capture photos of the interesting things you see. Write about your experience in your nature journal. Some ideas for where to go are:

1. Mountains
2. Desert
3. Ocean
4. Lake
5. Forest
6. Caves
7. Waterfalls
8. Marsh
9. State or national parks

Simple Ways to Enjoy Summer

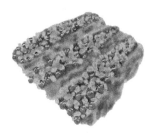

Plant a garden

Practice survival skills

Go for a walk

Watch the sunset

Go camping

Use a clothesline.

What if school looked like breakfasts in the backyard, library visits, family-led history lessons, more time with friends, or catching lightning bugs when the sun goes down?

Afterword

For many years, I struggled to find my rhythm in homeschooling. I tried out various methods and styles of teaching until stumbling upon the idea of slow living. I hadn't heard of that term before and was unknowingly already enjoying some of the aspects of the lifestyle while also yearning for the ones I didn't get to experience yet. Being obsessed with mimicking the school system and feeling concerned about what everyone else was doing was my weakness. I wanted my children to be involved in as many activities as possible and have a fully packed education. Getting ahead seemed like an appealing way for me as a mother to be successful.

After living like that for quite some time, I realized that I didn't want to rush my children through their days. I also didn't want to hurry to take care of our home or complete other necessary duties as a mother. I now refuse to be too busy to not be able to live slowly through this life that I have created. In a culture that rushes childhood, we are choosing to rebel by being more intentional with our time. The movement behind A Homemade Education is about intertwining a slowed-down home life with a child's education. It embraces family values, highlights quality time, and shines a positive light on learning together. Most of all, it recognizes the importance of being a kid in this ever-changing world and inspires mothers to create a wholesome childhood.

Other Books by the Author

Works Cited

Colonial Life: How Our Ancestors Lived During the 18th Century Jennifer Roger's. (2021, January 25). Medium.com

Screen Time and Children: MedlinePlus Medical Encyclopedia. (2023, April 25). MedlinePlus - Health Information from the National Library of Medicine. https://medlineplus.gov/ency/patientinstructions/000355.htm

Printed in Great Britain
by Amazon

46100189R00109